Measuring Up

to the

New York State Learning Standards

and Success Strategies for the State Test

English Language Arts

This book is customized for New York and the lessons match the New York State English Language Arts Learning Standards. The *Measuring Up* program includes comprehensive worktexts and New York Diagnostic Practice Tests which are available separately.

Level D

800-822-1080
www.NYStandardsHelp.com

PEOPLES PUBLISHING GROUP

299 Market Street, Saddle Brook, NJ 07663

Acknowledgments

Pg. 4, *Zabali and the Old Woman* reprinted by permission of *Spider* magazine, February, 1998, Vol. 5, No. 2, copyright © 1998 by Janet Nnakku Nsibambi; pg. 7, African American Museum photography, Courtesy of African American Museum, Hempstead, New York; pg. 11, *...If You Traveled West in a Covered Wagon* from IF YOU TRAVELED WEST IN A COVERED WAGON by Ellen Levine, illustrated by Elroy Freem. Text copyright © 1986 by Ellen Levine, illustrations copyright © 1992 by Scholastic Inc. Reprinted by permission of Scholastic, Inc.; pg. 19, *Puffins, Clowns of the Sea* reprinted by permission of *Spider* magazine, July, 1999, Vol. 6, No. 7, copyright © 1999 by Ruth J. Luhr; pg. 21, *Teddy's Bear* reprinted by permission of *Spider* magazine, May, 1998, No. 5, copyright © 1998 by Janeen R. Adil; pg. 28, *Welcome to the Rain Forest in Peru* from FACES, November 1997 issue: Peru: Life in a Rainforest copyright © 1998 by Scholastic Inc. and The New York Public Library, Astor, Lenox and Tilden Foundation. Reprinted by permission of Scholastic, Inc.; pg. 30, *The Internet* from The New York Public Library Kid's Guide to Research by Deborah Heiligman. Copyright © 1998 by Scholastic Inc. and The New York Public Library, Astor, Lenox and Tilden Foundation. Reprinted by permission of Scholastic, Inc.; pg. 42, *The Hungry Goddess* from *Momentos Magicos* by Olga Loya. Copyright 1997 by Olga Loya. Reprinted by permission of August House Publishers, Inc.; pg. 52, *Just Hang in There!* by Jim Janik, copyright © 1998, *Highlights for Children*, Inc., Columbus, Ohio; pg. 54, *Pa's Wonderful Girl* reprinted by permission of *Spider* magazine, June 1999, Vol. 6 No. 6, copyright © 1999 by Barbara N. Esposito; pg. 60, "Winter Moon" from *Collected Poems* by Langston Hughes copyright © 1994 by the Estate of Langston Hughes. Reprinted by permission of Alfred A. Knopf Inc.; pg. 61, *The Blues* from *Collected Poems* by Lanston Hughes copyright © 1994 by the Estate of Langston Hughes. Reprinted by permission of Alfred A. Knopf, Inc.; pg. 62, *The Owl and the Pussycat* by Edward Lear; pg. 64, "There's Always Weather" from *Collected Poems* by Langston Hughes Copyright © 1994 by the Estate of Langston Hughes. Reprinted by permission of Alfred A. Knopf, Inc.; pg. 177, *Grandma Moses: Making the Most of Life* by Pat McCarthy, copyright © 1998, Highlights for Children, Inc., Columbus, Ohio; photographs reprinted by permission, AP Wide World Photos, Archive Photos; pg. 183, *The Apple-Seed Man* by Paula Appling, copyright © 1998, Highlights for Children, Inc., Columbus, Ohio; pg. 207, From AUDUBON SOCIETY HOW WILDFLOWERS GET THEIR NAMES by Susan Hood. Published by Scholastic Reference, an imprint of Scholastic Inc. Copyright © 1998 by Chanticleer Press Inc. Reprinted by permission of Scholastic Inc.

The Peoples Publishing Group, Inc. expresses its thanks to all the people who helped to create this book.

Editorial Development, e2 Publishing Services
Pre-Press & Production Manager, Doreen Smith
Project Manager, Jason Grasso
Designer, Michele Sakow
Copy Editor and Proofreader, Pedra J. Del Vechio
Permissions Manager, Kristine Liebman
Cover Design, Cynthia Mackowicz, Michele Sakow, Yadiro Henriquez
Illustrator, Armando Baez
Publisher, Diane Miller

ISBN 1-56256-302-5

Copyright © 2000
The Peoples Publishing Group, Inc.
299 Market Street
Saddle Brook, New Jersey 07663-5312

Printed in the United States of America
20   19   18   17   16   15   14

Dear Student,

This year you will take a very important test in January. It is called the *New York State English Language Arts Test*. By preparing and practicing for this test—just like you would for an important game or performance—you will do well on it. The information and strategies in this book are designed to help you succeed on the test.

The test is given over three days. This is what it asks you to do:

Day 1   **45 minutes**
Read fiction and nonfiction passages and answer multiple-choice questions.

Day 2   **60 minutes**
Listen to a passage that is read aloud. Fill out a chart and write two short responses and one long response. The short responses are a few sentences long; the long response is a few paragraphs long.

Write a composition in response to a writing prompt.

Day 3   **60 minutes**
Read two linked passages. Fill out a chart and write two short responses and one long response.

In this book, there are times when you will be working with your teacher and times when you will be working independently. Here are some things you should know about the book.

 Look for this icon. It tells you that you are using the same format as the test. In each chapter, the first time you practice for a test, you will work with your teacher. Then you will practice independently.

 These lessons help you practice and review important skills you will need for the test.

Apply to the Test   These lessons show you how the skills you practiced apply to the test. It puts these skills in the test format.

 These activities can be completed at home. Take your book home and share what you are learning with your family.

Now it's time to get started. By the time you finish this book, you'll be ready and able for the test. Good luck!

Dear Caregiver,

No doubt you want to help your child succeed in school. One of the key ways success is measured is by standardized tests. This book will help prepare your child for success on the *New York State English Language Arts Test*. It was developed specifically for New York State and is aligned with the New York State standards.

The *New York State English Language Arts Test* is given in January over three days. Here is what happens each day.

Day 1   **45 minutes**
Students read fiction and nonfiction passages and answer multiple-choice questions.

Day 2   **60 minutes**
Students listen to a passage that is read aloud. They fill out a chart and write two short responses and one long response. The short responses are a few sentences long; the long response is a few paragraphs long.

Students write a composition in response to a writing prompt.

Day 3   **60 minutes**
Students read two linked passages. They fill out a chart and write two short responses and one long response.

Measuring Up on the New York State English Language Arts Test is the ideal tool for your child to use to review, practice, and prepare for the test. The information and the strategies also will help your child be successful in day-to-day schoolwork.

Measuring Up on the New York State English Language Arts Test prepares your child to master the skills covered each day on the test. It provides practice in the actual test formats—first using a guided practice and then an independent practice. This test practice will help your child feel more confident when the actual day of the test arrives. This book is not easy, but then neither is the test! New York State expects its students to measure up to the standards.

Your involvement is a crucial factor in your child's success. As we begin each chapter, I will send home a letter telling you what your child will be learning. From time to time, your child will bring home an activity to complete. This activity will take only a short time to complete, but by working together with your child, you will show that you think his or her success on the test is important.

Here are some other things you might do to help your child be successful:

Read Aloud to Your Child
Find a quiet space to read to your child. Share books you loved as a child. Read stories you hold dear, both fiction and nonfiction. As you read, talk about the story with your child.

Talk About What You Read or Hear Together
Talk about events in the news. Listen to a news report together and discuss the information. Read the newspaper with your child and talk about articles of interest.

Use Environmental Print
Things to read are all around us. Get in the habit of pointing out things to read in the supermarket. Have your child read labels on products and signs giving directions. When your child gets a new game or toy, read the directions together. When you plan a trip, read a map together and work out an itinerary. Have your child write or phone a tourist bureau for brochures.

Show That You Think Reading Is Important
Let your child see you reading. Bring home memos from work. Read magazines and newspapers. Talk about the books you are reading. Visit bookstores and the library with your child. If you have a computer and are hooked up to the Internet, "surf the net" together.

If you have any questions regarding the test or your child's progress, please don't hesitate to get in touch with me.

Table of Contents

Day 1

UNIT 1

READING FOR MEANING 1

Day 2 & 3

UNIT 2
WRITING TO DEMONSTRATE UNDERSTANDING 68

Correlation to the New York State Learning Standards and Major Understandings

This worktext is customized to the *New York English Language Arts Core Curriculum* and will help you prepare for the *New York State Test in English Language Arts for Grade 4.*

After the lesson is completed, place a (✓) to indicate Mastery or an (✗) to indicate Review Needed.

Standard 1: Reading

	U1	1	2	U2	3	4	5	6
WHAT STUDENTS READ, Grades 2–4, for Information and Understanding								
Read from informational texts, such as: books, biographies, age-appropriate reference materials, children's magazines/newspapers, and electronic-based texts, such as encyclopedias.	O						O	O
WHAT STUDENT DO FOR INFORMATION AND UNDERSTANDING: the competencies that 2–4 students demonstrate as they learn to read include to:								
Locate and use library media resources, with assistance, to acquire information		O			O	O	O	O
Read unfamiliar texts independently to collect and interpret data, facts, and ideas		O	O			O	O	O
Read and understand written directions	O	O	O			O	O	O
Locate information in a text that is needed to solve a problem		O						
Identify main ideas and supporting details in informational texts		O	O				O	O
Recognize and use organizational features of texts, such as table of contents, indexes, page numbers, and chapter headings/subheadings to locate information		O						
Relate data and facts from informational texts to prior information and experience	O	O	O					O
Compare and contrast information on one topic from two different sources				O	O	O		O
Identify a conclusion that summarizes the main idea		O	O					O
Select books independently to meet informational needs		O			O			
Identify and interpret significant facts taken from maps, graphs, charts, and other visuals		O						
Use graphic organizers to record significant details from informational texts.		O				O		O
WHAT STUDENTS DO ACROSS ALL FOUR ENGLISH LANGUAGE ARTS STANDARDS: The competencies that 2–4 students demonstrate as they learn to read include to:								
Identify purpose for reading		O						O
Use letter-sound correspondence, knowledge of grammar, and overall context to determine meaning	O	O	O		O	O		
Use decoding strategies, such as sounding out words, comparing similar words, breaking words into smaller words, and looking for word parts (root words, prefixes, and suffixes)		O						
Use self-monitoring strategies, such as re reading and cross-checking	O	O	O					O
Apply corrective strategies, using classroom resources such as teachers, peers, and reference tools					O			
Recognize the difference between phrases and sentences			O		O			
Read with attention to sentence structure and punctuation, such as periods, question marks, and commas to assist in comprehension			O					
Engage in independent silent reading		O						
Locate the name of the author, illustrator, the title page, table of contents, index, and chapter headings	O	O	O		O			O
Recognize and discriminate among a variety of informational texts		O						O
Determine the meaning of unfamiliar words by using context clues, dictionaries, and other classroom resources	O	O	O		O		O	O
Read aloud at appropriate rate		O	O			O		
Read with increasing fluency and confidence from a variety of texts	O	O	O	O		O	O	O
Maintain a personal reading list to reflect reading goals and accomplishments			O			O	O	
Use computer software to support reading	O	O	O					

Standard 1: Writing

	U1	1	2	U2	3	4	5	6
WHAT STUDENTS WRITE, Grades 2–4, for Information and Understanding								
Write the following in order to begin to transmit information: short reports of several paragraphs to two pages, brief summaries, graphs and charts, concept maps and semantic webs, simple outlines, formal letters, simple directions.					O			O
WHAT STUDENTS DO ACROSS ALL FOUR ENGLISH LANGUAGE ARTS STANDARDS: The competencies that 2-4 students demonstrate as they learn to write include to:								

This worktext is customized to the *New York English Language Arts Core Curriculum* and will help you prepare for the *New York State Test in English Language Arts for Grade 4.*

After the lesson is completed, place a (✓) to indicate Mastery or an (✗) to indicate Review Needed.

Standard 1: Writing (continued) Mastered Skill / Review Skill / Lessons	U1	1	2	U2	3	4	5	6
Use at least two sources of information in writing a report	O					O		O
Take notes to record data, facts, and ideas, both by following teacher direction and by writing independently					O	O	O	
State a main idea and support it with facts and details		O		O	O	O	O	O
Use organizational patterns for expository writing, such as compare/contrast, cause/effect, and time/order					O	O	O	O
Connect personal experiences and observations to new information from school subject are as					O	O	O	O
Use dictionaries and/or computer software to spell words correctly	O			O	O		O	O
Produce clear, well-organized, and well-developed explanations, reports, accounts, and directions that demonstrate understanding of a topic	O			O	O	O	O	O
Support interpretations and explanations with evidence from text				O	O	O	O	O
Maintain a portfolio that includes informational writing as a method of reviewing work with teachers and parents/caregivers .					O			
WHAT STUDENTS DO ACROSS ALL FOUR ENGLISH LANGUAGE ARTS STANDARDS: The competencies that 2–4 students demonstrate as they learn to write include to:								
Begin to develop a voice in writing		O			O	O	O	
Spell frequently used words correctly					O	O	O	O
Use basic punctuation correctly, such as commas, periods, exclamation points, and question marks		O			O	O	O	O
Use correct verb tense					O	O	O	O
Use varied vocabulary and sentence structure					O	O	O	O
Write sentences in logical order and create paragraphs to develop ideas					O	O	O	O
Use an organizational format that reflects a beginning, middle, and end				O	O	O	O	O
Develop an idea within a brief text .					O	O	O	O
Learn and use the "writing process" (prewriting, drafting, revising, proofreading)					O	O	O	O
Use revision strategies to develop writing, including conferring with teachers and peers, and cut and paste					O	O	O	O
Determine the intended audience before writing					O		O	
Use legible print and/or cursive writing								O
Use word processing.					O			

Standard 1: Listening Mastered Skill / Review Skill / Lessons	U1	1	2	U2	3	4	5	6
WHAT STUDENTS LISTEN TO, Grades 2–4, for Information and Understanding								
Listen for data, facts, and ideas in, for example: small and large group discussions, conferences with teachers, school assemblies, student presentations, multimedia presentations, oral readings.	O							
WHAT STUDENTS DO FOR INFORMATION AND UNDERSTANDING: The competencies that 2–4 students demonstrate as they learn to listen include to:								
Listen in order to: acquire information and/or understand procedures, identify essential details, determine the sequence of steps given, identify main ideas and supporting details, identify a conclusion that summarizes the main idea, interpret information by drawing on prior knowledge and experience, collect information.	O	O		O	O	O		
WHAT STUDENTS DO ACROSS ALL FOUR ENGLISH LANGUAGE ARTS STANDARDS: The competencies that 2–4 students demonstrate as they learn to listen include to:								
Listen respectfully and responsively					O	O		O
Attend to a listening activity for an extended period of time			O		O	O		
Avoid interrupting					O	O		O
Respond appropriately to what is heard.					O	O		

This worktext is customized to the *New York English Language Arts Core Curriculum* and will help you prepare for the *New York State Test in English Language Arts for Grade 4.*

After the lesson is completed, place a (✓) to indicate Mastery or an (✗) to indicate Review Needed.

Standard 1: Speaking	Mastered Skill Review Skill							
Lessons	U1	1	2	U2	3	4	5	6
WHEN STUDENTS SPEAK, Grades 2–4, for Information and Understanding								
Speak to share data, facts, and ideas in, for example: small group interactions, class discussions and meetings, conferences with teachers, classroom presentations, read-aloud situations.		O						
WHAT STUDENTS DO FOR INFORMATION AND UNDERSTANDING: The competencies that 2–4 students demonstrate as they learn to speak include to:								
Speak in order to: provide directions, express an opinion, ask questions, summarize, provide a sequence of steps, describe a problem and suggest one or more solutions, state a main idea with supporting examples and details, explain a line of reasoning.	O				O	O	O	O
Present a short oral report, using at least two sources of information, such as a person, a book, a magazine article, a television program, or electronic text								
Use complete sentences, age- and content-appropriate vocabulary								
Use logical order in presentations.					O			
WHAT STUDENTS DO ACROSS ALL FOUR ENGLISH LANGUAGE ARTS STANDARDS: The competencies that 2–4 students demonstrate as they learn to speak include to:								
Respond respectfully		O	O		O		O	
Initiate communication with peers and familiar adults		O	O		O	O	O	
Use age-appropriate vocabulary					O			
Speak in grammatically correct sentences					O			
Use gestures appropriate to conveying meaning		O	O		O	O		
Establish eye contact to engage the audience		O			O	O		O
Speak loudly enough to be heard by the audience.		O			O	O		O

Standard 2: Students will read, write, listen, and speak for literary response and expression. Reading	Mastered Skill Review Skill							
Lessons	U1	1	2	U2	3	4	5	6
WHAT STUDENTS READ, Grades 2–4, for Literary Response and Expression								
Read and view imaginative texts and performances, such as: stories, poems and songs, folktales and fables, plays, film and video productions, electronic books		O						
WHAT STUDENTS DO FOR LITERARY RESPONSE AND EXPRESSION: The competencies that 2–4 students demonstrate as they learn to read include to:								
Select literature based on personal needs and interests from a variety of genres and by different authors		O						
Engage in purposeful oral reading in small and large groups		O				O		
Read print-based and electronic imaginative texts silently on a daily basis for enjoyment		O	O	O				
Recognize the diff e rences among the genres of stories, poems, and plays				O				O
Relate setting, plot, and characters in literature to own lives	O							
Explain the difference between fiction and nonfiction		O	O					O
Use previous reading and life experiences to understand and compare literature	O		O					O
Make predictions, and draw conclusions and inferences about events and characters	O	O	O					O
Identify cultural influences in texts and performances	O	O						O
Recognize the value of illustration in imaginative text			O					
Maintain a personal reading list to reflect reading accomplishments and goals			O				O	
Use specific evidence from stories to identify themes; describe characters, their actions and motivations; and relate sequences of events			O					O
Use knowledge of story structure, story elements, and key vocabulary to interpret stories	O		O			O		O
Use graphic organizers to record significant details about characters and events in stories.			O			O		O

This worktext is customized to the *New York English Language Arts Core Curriculum* and will help you prepare for the *New York State Test in English Language Arts for Grade 4.*

After the lesson is completed, place a (✓) to indicate Mastery or an (✗) to indicate Review Needed.

Standard 2: Writing

	U1	1	2	U2	3	4	5	6
WHAT STUDENTS WRITE, Grades 2–4, for Literary Response and Expression								
Write original imaginative texts, such as: stories, poems and songs, plays				○				
Write adaptations				○				
Write interpretive and responsive essays of a few paragraphs.							○	
WHAT STUDENTS DO FOR LITERARY RESPONSE AND EXPRESSION: The competencies that 2–4 students demonstrate as the learn to write include to:								
Write original imaginative texts: create characters, simple plot and setting, use rhythm and rhyme to create short poems and songs, use dialogue to create short plays, use vivid and playful language, use descriptive language to create an image,			○			○		
Write interpretive and responsive essays in order to, for example: identify title, author, and illustrator, describe literary elements such as plot, setting, characters, describe themes of imaginative texts, express a personal response to literature, compare and contrast elements of text					○	○	○	○
Produce clear, well-organized responses to stories read or listened to, supporting the understanding of themes, characters, and events with details from story				○		○	○	○
Produce imaginative stories and personal narratives that show insight, development, organization, and effective language						○	○	○
Use resources such as personal experiences and themes from other texts and performances to stimulate own writing					○	○	○	○
Use a computer to create, respond to, and interpret imaginative texts					○			
Maintain a portfolio that includes imaginative and interpretive writing as a method of reviewing work with teachers and parents/caregivers.					○			

Standard 2: Listening

	U1	1	2	U2	3	4	5	6
WHAT STUDENTS LISTEN TO, Grades 2–4, for Literary Response and Expression								
Listen to comprehend, interpret, and respond to imaginative texts and performances, such as: stories, poems and songs, folktales and fables, plays, and films and video productions.						○		
WHAT STUDENTS DO FOR LITERARY RESPONSE AND EXPRESSION: The competencies that 2–4 students demonstrate as they learn to listen include to:								
Listen in order to: identify elements of character, plot, and setting to understand author's message or intent, connect imaginative texts to previous reading and life experiences to enhance understanding and appreciation, identify author's use of rhythm, repetition, and rhyme, compare and contrast ideas of others to own ideas					○	○		
Use note taking and webbing strategies to organize information and ideas recalled from stories read aloud.			○		○	○		

Standard 2: Speaking

	U1	1	2	U2	3	4	5	6
WHEN STUDENTS SPEAK, Grades 2–4, for Literary Response and Expression								
Speak to present interpretations and responses to imaginative texts in, for example: class and group discussions, role play and creative drama, conferences with teacher, book reviews.						○		
WHAT STUDENTS DO FOR LITERARY RESPONSE AND EXPRESSION: The competencies that 2–4 students demonstrate as they learn to speak include to:								
Speak in order to: present original works such as stories, poems, and plays to classmates; give book reviews; describe characters, setting, and plot; make inferences and draw conclusions; compare imaginative texts and performances to personal experiences and prior knowledge; explain cultural and ethnic features in imaginative texts; ask questions to clarify and interpret imaginative texts and performances; discuss themes of imaginative texts.			○		○	○	○	○
Use complete sentences, correct verb tense, age-appropriate vocabulary, and logical order in oral presentation.					○			○

Copying is illegal.

Measuring Up™ to the New York State Learning Standards

This worktext is customized to the *New York English Language Arts Core Curriculum* and will help you prepare for the *New York State Test in English Language Arts for Grade 4.*

After the lesson is completed, place a (✓) to indicate Mastery or an (✗) to indicate Review Needed.

Standard 3: Students will read, write, listen, and speak for critical analysis and evaluation. Reading	Mastered Skill / Review Skill Lessons	U1	1	2	U2	3	4	5	6
WHAT STUDENTS READ, Grades 2–4, for Critical Analysis and Evaluation									
Read to analyze and evaluate information, ideas, and experiences from resources, such as: children's books, children's articles, editorials in student newspapers, advertisements, and electronic resources.							○		
WHAT STUDENTS DO FOR CRITICAL ANALYSIS AND EVALUATION: The competencies that 2–4 students demonstrate as they learn to read include to:									
Evaluate the content by identifying: the author's purpose; important and unimportant details; whether events, actions, characters, and/or settings are realistic; and recurring themes across works in print and media				○		○			○
Compare and contrast characters, plot, and setting in two literary works				○					○
Analyze ideas and information based on prior knowledge and personal experience		○	○			○			○
Recognize how language and illustrations are used to persuade in printed and filmed advertisements and texts such as letters to the editor							○		
Judge truthfulness or accuracy of content with assistance from teachers and parents/caregivers in order to gather facts and form opinions							○		○
Use opinions and reactions of teachers and classmates to evaluate personal interpretation of ideas, information, and experience.				○		○		○	

Standard 3: Writing	Mastered Skill / Review Skill Lessons	U1	1	2	U2	3	4	5	6
WHAT STUDENTS WRITE, Grades 2–4, for Critical Analysis and Evaluation									
Write the following to analyze and evaluate ideas, information, and experiences: persuasive essays, editorials for classroom and school newspapers, movie and book reviews, reports and essays, and advertisements.								○	
WHAT STUDENTS DO FOR CRITICAL ANALYSIS AND EVALUATION: The competencies that 2–4 students demonstrate as they learn to write include to:									
Use prewriting tools such as semantic webs and concept maps to organize ideas and information				○		○	○	○	
State a main idea, theme, or opinion and provide supporting details from the text					○	○	○	○	○
Use relevant examples, reasons, and explanations to support ideas						○	○	○	○
Express opinions and make judgments that demonstrate a personal point of view							○	○	○
Use personal experiences and knowledge to analyze and valuate new ideas								○	○
Analyze and evaluate the author's use of setting, plot, character, rhyme, rhythm, and language in written and visual text				○				○	○
Create an advertisement, using words and pictures, in order to illustrate an opinion about a product				○			○	○	
Use effective vocabulary in persuasive and expository writing							○	○	
Use details from stories or informational texts to predict, explain, or show relationships between information and events						○	○	○	○
Use ideas from two or more sources of information to generalize about causes, effects, or other relationships						○		○	○
Maintain a portfolio that includes written analysis and evaluation as a method of reviewing work with teachers and parents/caregivers.						○		○	

This worktext is customized to the *New York English Language Arts Core Curriculum* and will help you prepare for the *New York State Test in English Language Arts for Grade 4.*

After the lesson is completed, place a (✓) to indicate Mastery or an (✗) to indicate Review Needed.

Standard 3: Listening	Mastered Skill								
	Review Skill								
	Lessons	U1	1	2	U2	3	4	5	6
WHAT STUDENTS LISTEN TO, Grades 2–4, for Critical analysis and Evaluation									
Listen to analyze and evaluate ideas, information, and experiences in, for example: class and group discussions; conferences with teacher; role plays; classroom presentations, such as oral book reviews; and individual or group viewing of advertisements, videos, and movies.						O			
WHAT STUDENTS DO FOR CRITICAL ANALYSIS AND EVALUATION: The competencies that 2–4 students demonstrate as they learn to listen include to:									
Listen in order to: distinguish between information in media texts such as live action news coverage, and fictional material in dramatic productions; form a personal opinion about the quality of texts read aloud based on criteria such as characters, plot, and setting; recognize the perspectives of others; form an opinion about the message of advertisements, based on the language; distinguish between fact and opinion; and evaluate the speaker's style of delivery by using criteria such as volume and tone of voice.				O		O	O		

Standard 3: Speaking	Mastered Skill								
	Review Skill								
	Lessons	U1	1	2	U2	3	4	5	6
WHEN STUDENTS SPEAK, Grades 2–4, for Critical Analysis and Evaluation									
Speak to express opinions and judgments in, for example: class and group discussions; role plays; conferences with teacher; book reviews; and presentations.			O						
WHAT STUDENTS DO FOR CRITICAL ANALYSIS AND EVALUATION: The competencies that 2–4 students demonstrate as they learn to speak include to:									
Speak in order to: explain the reasons for a character's actions, considering both the situation and the motivation of the character; express an opinion or judgment about a character, setting, and plot in a variety of works; discuss the impact of vocabulary, format, illustrations, and titles in evaluating ideas, information, and experiences; express an opinion or judgment about school or community issues; use personal experience and knowledge to analyze and evaluate new ideas; express an opinion about the accuracy and truthfulness of the content of literary works, editorials, reviews, and advertisements supported by the text; role play to communicate an interpretation or evaluation of real or imaginary people or events; ask and respond to questions; use appropriate eye contact and gestures in presentations and responses; speak with appropriate rate and volume for the audience; and take turns speaking in a group.			O	O		O	O	O	O

Measuring Up™ to the New York State Learning Standards

READING FOR MEANING

What's Expected on the New York State English Language Arts Test?

It's Day 1 of the New York State English Language Arts Test. What is going to happen? What you are going to be expected to do?

First, you will read three to five passages. Some of these passages will be nonfiction. Nonfiction is writing that contains information about real things, real people, and real events. Helen Keller's book about her own life is nonfiction.

Some of these passages will be fiction. Fiction is imaginative literature about made-up people and made-up events. *The Wizard of Oz* by Frank L. Baum is fiction.

Next, you will answer multiple-choice questions. These questions test that you have understood what you have read. They show that you can:

* **Read both fiction and nonfiction**
* **Understand important ideas and information**
* **Recognize what makes a good story**
* **Figure out the meaning of words you do not know**

So get ready to show your stuff! The information and practice in this book will help you put your best foot forward and show what you really know.

Keys to Success

These strategies will help you read both fiction and nonfiction. They will help you ace the test.

Ask Questions

Stop and ask yourself questions about what you read. For example, if you were reading about the Oregon Trail, you might ask questions like these:

Where did the Oregon Trail begin?
What were some of the dangers people faced?
Why did people want to travel to Oregon?

Then read on to find answers to your own questions.

Make It Clear

Take time to make sure you understand the information. Clear up anything that confuses you. Here are some things that might confuse you as your read.

Confusion You don't know the meaning of a word.

WHAT TO DO
- Look the word up in a dictionary.
- Use context clues to figure out the meaning.

Confusion The author mentions a person, place, or event that you do not know.

WHAT TO DO
- See if the author explains this information later in the passage.
- Look for a footnote at the bottom of the page giving you more information.
- If both these strategies fail, look up the person, place, or event in an encyclopedia or dictionary.

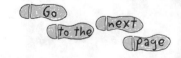

Keys to Success

Summarize

Summarize as you read. When you give a summary, you give the main points. You leave out all the extra details. Summarizing will help you keep track of the content.

Predict

Make predictions or guesses about what you think will happen next. Then read on to see if your predictions are correct. You might even discuss what you are reading with friends. See if they make the same predictions as you.

Connect

Connect what you read to what you already know. Have you ever done something like the characters in the story are doing? Have you ever been to a place similar to the one the author describes?

Form Pictures

Form mental pictures as you read. Try to see the people and events with your mind's eye. For example, if the author writes about a snake, form a mental picture of the way the snake moves and what it looks like. When the author describes a character, picture what this character looks like.

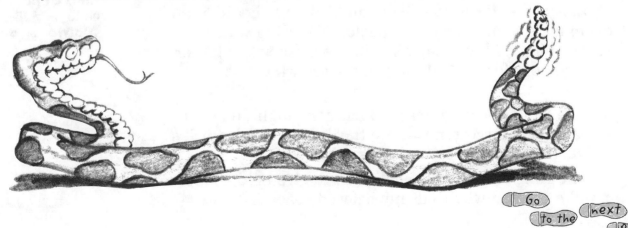

Go to the next page

Directions Put your key strategies to work as you read the following story. The questions on the side will help you.

❶

Zabali and the Old Woman
Janet Nnakku Nsibambi

❷ Once upon a time, on the plains of East Africa, there lived a mighty king. One day he went out hunting with his son and many servants. But he did not catch any animals, and he was so angry, his servants didn't know what to do.

❸ On the way back to the palace, the King ordered everyone to stop. He was sure he had seen something moving in the brush. He pulled out his spear, but before he could throw it, a baby peacock limped toward him. The poor little thing had lost its mother, and its leg hurt.

❹ No longer angry, the King dropped his spear and picked up the little bird. He took it home and had his servants build a fancy house for it. The King loved the peacock so much that only he and his son were allowed to feed it. The peacock's leg healed, and the bird grew big and strong. Its **❺** feathers were bright and beautiful.

Now, in the same village, there lived a young boy named Zabali. His family was very poor. They had only one hen, **❻** one milk cow, and a small *shamba*, or garden, where they grew vegetables.

❼ Nearby lived an old woman. Every morning Zabali would carry water for her from the river. Every evening he would bring her firewood. He gave her eggs from his family's hen, milk from the cow, and vegetables from the garden. The Old Woman was so grateful, but she had nothing to give Zabali in return.

Early one morning, Zabali and his family heard loud drumbeats coming from the palace. The King was summoning all the villagers. Zabali's mother and father jumped out of their beds and ran to see what was happening.

The King was very upset. During the night, one of his servants had forgotten to close the door to the peacock's house, and now the peacock was lost.

The King said to the people, "I will give land and many cows to the one who finds my beloved peacock."

Guided Questions

❶ Read the title and author's name. Can you *predict* where this story takes place?

❷ *Check your prediction.* Where does this story take place? Were you right?

❸ Try to *picture* the peacock in your mind. How do you think it looked?

❹ This is a good place to *ask a question* about the King. Why did he drop his spear? What do his actions tell you about him?

❺ Stop here to *summarize*. What has happened so far in this story?

❻ *Shamba* is an African word. Make sure you are *clear* about what it means. What does it mean?

❼ *Connect* Zabali to your own life. Can you think of people who are kind like Zabali is? Can you think of people who need help like the Old Woman does?

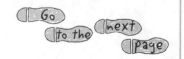
Go to the next page

8 And with that, he ordered the villagers to start searching. Zabali's father and mother went home and told Zabali what the King had said.

Before they began to search, Zabali said, "I must take some water to my friend, the Old Woman."

The Old Woman was happy to see Zabali. She asked him about the drums. Zabali told her that the King's peacock was missing.

The Old Woman said, "There is a beautiful bird behind my house. It came last night, and I've been feeding it rice. Could it be the King's peacock?"

Zabali went with the Old Woman to look at the bird. Its feathers were so bright and beautiful!

9 The Old Woman said, "Please take it for being kind to me."

Zabali put the bird in a big basket and ran to the King's palace. The King's guards asked him what he wanted.

"I want to see the King!" said Zabali.

"No one can see the King now. He is too upset. Go away!"

10 Zabali insisted. "Please let me see the King. Maybe I can make him happy again." The guards just laughed.

When the King heard his guards laughing, he was very angry. "How can you laugh when I am so miserable?" he asked.

The guards told him, "There is a small boy here who thinks he can make you happy!"

When the King saw Zabali and his big basket, he was very curious. But Zabali was so excited to be standing near the King that he couldn't even speak. Instead, he opened the basket, and the peacock jumped out. It ran straight to the King.

11 The King was so pleased that he gave Zabali some of his best land, a big house, and many cows, goats, and chickens. Zabali's family was no longer poor, and they invited the Old Woman to live with them. She was never alone again.

12 That is the end of my story.

8 Make a *prediction* here. What do you think will happen next? Read on to see if you are right.

9 Stop here to *summarize* what has happened in this part of the story.

10 *Question* the guards behavior. Why did they laugh?

11 Did this story turn out as you thought it would? Explain your answer.

12 Have you read other stories like this? Tell about them.

Chapter 1 INFORMATIONAL TEXT

What's It All About?

In this chapter, you will learn

🟤 what is informational text

🟤 strategies for reading informational text

🟤 how to answer multiple choice questions

🟤 how to find main ideas and supporting details

🟤 how to understand conclusions

🟤 how to read maps, graphs, charts

🟤 how to use context clues

Have you ever been in one of these situations?

1. You are writing a report on American Indian tribes in New York State. You need to find information.

2. You want to build a model airplane. You need directions on how to do this.

3. You like to talk about baseball with your friends. You need information about your favorite team and players.

Places To Find Information

Information is all around us.

✱ Visit the art museum in your town. You can find information about famous artists and their paintings.

✱ Visit a natural history museum. You can find information about how animals live.

✱ At the aquarium, you can discover facts about fish and other creatures that live under water.

Go to the next page

ACTIVITY

Directions The chart below contains places in New York State you can visit or write to for information. What information do you think you can find at each place? Write your answer in the right-hand column. Compare your answers with those of your classmates. The first one is done for you.

Buffalo and Erie City Historical Society Buffalo, New York	1. *Information about the history of western New York.*
National Soccer Hall of Fame Oneonta, New York	2.
Hispanic Society of America New York, New York	3.
Museum of Colonial History Narrowsburg, New York	4.
Iroquois Indian Museum Howe's Cave, New York	5.
National Baseball Hall of Fame Cooperstown, New York	6.
Franklin Delano Roosevelt Home and Library Hyde Park, New York	7.
Lake George Zoological Park Queensbury, New York	8.
Rochester Museum of Science Rochester, New York	9.
African-American Museum Hempstead, New York	10.

LESSON 1   What Is Informational Text?

Informational text contains information about the real world. It provides facts about real-life things, real-life people, and real-life events. For example, informational text may tell about

* wildlife in the Adirondacks
* how New York Yankee Roger Clemens won five Cy Young Awards
* the role New York played in the Revolutionary War
* how to make a teepee

Forms of Information

Information comes in all forms. Here are some forms of information you read and listen to every day.

Print
Biographies
Reference Books
Magazines
Newspapers
Brochures

Non-Print
Newscasts
Documentaries
Historical Movies
Television Biographies
Historic Villages

Electronic Media
CD-Rom Encyclopedias
CD-Rom Dictionaries
Websites
Internet
e-mail

ACTIVITY

Directions Think about all the things you have read and listened to for information. Then brainstorm to create a list of as many forms of information as you can. Stretch your mind. Of course, you will include books. But also try to include some unusual items. List labels on products. List information on the back of cereal boxes. Include information on place mats in restaurants, for example. Share your list with your classmates.

_____

_____

_____

_____

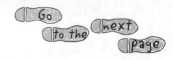

Go to the next page

Measuring Up™ to the New York State Learning Standards

Reference Books

● ● ● ● ● ● ● ● ● ● ● ● ●

Your library or school media center contains many reference books for you to use to find information. Some are even available in electronic format. Here are some books you might use.

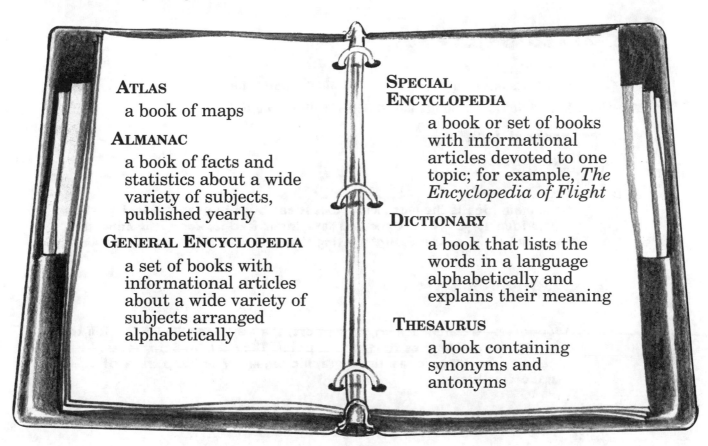

ATLAS
a book of maps

ALMANAC
a book of facts and statistics about a wide variety of subjects, published yearly

GENERAL ENCYCLOPEDIA
a set of books with informational articles about a wide variety of subjects arranged alphabetically

SPECIAL ENCYCLOPEDIA
a book or set of books with informational articles devoted to one topic; for example, *The Encyclopedia of Flight*

DICTIONARY
a book that lists the words in a language alphabetically and explains their meaning

THESAURUS
a book containing synonyms and antonyms

ACTIVITY

Directions Your job is to find the following information. **What resource would you use for each?**

1. the most recent population count for Rochester, New York _____

2. a word that means the opposite of *problem* _____

3. a map of New York State _____

4. the meaning of the word *environment* _____

5. information about the French and Indian War _____

LESSON 2 How to Read Informational Text

On Day 1 of the *New York State English Language Arts Test*, you will read three to five passages. Then you will answer 28 multiple choice questions about these passages. Some of the passages contain informational text.

Keys to Success

These strategies will help you be successful when reading informational text. On page 11, you will see how to put these strategies to work.

When you read, look for

Main Idea

The main idea is the most important idea about the topic. Identify the main idea as you read. Once you have identified it, keep it in mind as you finish the passage. Highlighting the main idea may help you do this.

Supporting Details

Supporting details back up, or support, the main idea. Pay attention to the details the author uses to make the point. They can be data, facts, reasons, and other ideas. Use a graphic organizer to keep track of supporting ideas.

Conclusion That Summarizes the Main Idea

Sometimes the author ends the passage by again stating the most important idea. But this time, the main idea is stated in different words. By beginning with the main idea and stating it again at the end, the author makes the point even more strongly.

Maps, Graphs, and Charts

Informational articles often contain more than just print. They may include maps, graphs, and charts to provide key information.

Context

You may not know the meaning of a word. Look at the topic of the passage and the other words surrounding the unknown word. They may provide clues that help you figure out the meaning.

 Measuring Up™ to the New York State Learning Standards

READING GUIDE

Directions Put your reading strategies to work as you read this passage from **...If You Traveled West in a Covered Wagon.** The questions and comments on the right will help you.

❶ *from*
...If You Traveled West in a Covered Wagon
Ellen Levine

❷ One hundred and fifty years ago there was no railroad that went all across the country. There were no cars or buses or airplanes. The only way to travel across the country was to ride a horse, or if you went with your family, to travel in a covered wagon.

❸ ❹ In the 1840s and 1850s, thousands of people traveled west. So if you lived at that time, there was a chance you might have traveled in a covered wagon.

What was the Oregon Territory?

In the 1840s the Oregon Territory was made up of the land that is now the states of Oregon, Washington, Idaho, and parts of Montana and Wyoming.

Back then nobody knew if the Oregon Territory was going to be part of America or if it was going to be part of England. Both countries had built forts in the territory. At the forts, trappers and Indians sold animal furs and skins, such as beaver, marten, and muskrat, and bought tools and supplies.

❺ America and England agreed that Oregon would belong to the country that could get more of its people living in the new land. So to make Oregon part of America, many Americans had to go there to live. Oregon finally became a state in 1859.

Why did some people want to travel all the way to Oregon?

❻ Back in the 1840s, you heard about far away places by reading the newspaper or hearing stories told by visitors who came from distant places. This is how people learned of a land on the other side—the west side—of the Rocky Mountains. That land was called *Oregon*.

❶ The title tells you the *topic*, or what the passage is about. What is the topic? When do you think the events in this passage happened? Why?

❷ This paragraph tells you the *main idea*. What is the most important idea?

❸ *Picture* traveling this way. What hardships do you think people faced?

❹ Check your *prediction*. Were you right about when the events happened?

❺ This paragraph gives a *reason* why so many Americans had to travel to the Oregon Territory. What is the reason?

❻ *Connect* this information with your own life. How do you learn about distant lands today?

Go to the next page

Stories told about Oregon made it sound like a magical place. Flowers bloomed all year. The land was good for farming. And there was plenty of land that you could get for free. There were tall trees and big forests, and rivers and streams filled with fish.

7 So the very name *Oregon* made people think of starting new adventures.

What was a covered wagon?

8 A covered wagon was a wagon with a white rounded top made of cloth. The cloth was called canvas and was rubbed with oil to make it waterproof. It was stretched over big wooden hoops that were bent from one side of the wagon to the other.

There were drawstrings in the front and the back of the canvas. If you pulled the strings tight, you could close the ends up to keep out the rain or wind. The canvas could also be rolled up on the long sides, so that you could get a breeze on a hot day.

The bottom part of the covered wagon looked like an ordinary wagon with one difference: The front wheels were smaller than the back wheels. That made it easier to make sharp turns.

Inside the wagon there were hooks on the wooden hoops. On them you could hang milk cans, guns, bonnets, spoons, dolls, jackets, and anything else there was room for. Underneath the wagon between the back wheels there was a hook with a bucket of grease hanging down from it. The grease was rubbed on the wheels so that they would turn smoothly.

In the front of the wagon there was a wooden board to sit on.

The covered wagon was pulled by oxen or mules or horses. Many pioneers used oxen because they were stronger than mules and horses.

Covered wagons were also called prairie schooners. Can you guess why?

9 A schooner is a boat that sails on the seas. The big white canvas cover on the wagon looked like a huge sail. And if the grass was tall enough to hide the wheels, the wagon looked like a big boat sailing across the grassy green waves.

7 *Summarize* the reasons people wanted to travel to Oregon.

8 Notice all the *details* you learn here. How did people protect themselves from rain?

9 Use *context* to explain the meaning of prairie schooner. Can you *picture* lines of prairie schooners sailing across the prairies?

Prepare for the Test

Amultiple choice question has two parts. The first part is the question itself. This part usually has a number before it. The second part is the four choices. These have letters in front of them. Only one choice is right.

Directions
Read the sample multiple choice question. Then look at the strategies.

SAMPLE MULTIPLE CHOICE QUESTION

1 The main idea of this paragraph is that Joe DiMaggio is a baseball legend. Which of the following statements does NOT support this main idea?

A He holds the record for an unbroken string of games with a hit.
B He died of lung cancer.
C While Joe was on their team, the Yankees won the World Series nine times.
D His career batting average is .325.

Test Taking Strategies

Find Key Words

Read the question (the part before the choices) carefully. Look for key words that tell you what to do. In the sample above, the key words are "NOT support the main idea." Notice that the word NOT is in capital letters. This tells you to watch out. Don't be tricked.

Read All Choices First

The choices have letters in front of them. Read all the choices first. Three of the choices will support the main idea. Only one of them will not. This is the one you are to pick.

Reread the Choices

Go through the choices one by one. In the sample above, you know that A supports the main idea. C and D also support the main idea. The correct answer has to be B.

Mark Your Answer

Mark your answer. Fill in only one answer. If you have to erase, make sure you erase completely. If two letters are marked, your answer will be marked incorrect.

Go On

SAMPLE TEST

Multiple Choice Questions

D*irections*
Answer these questions about "…If You Traveled West in a Covered Wagon."

1 How did most families travel to the West in the 1840s and 1850s?

   A by airplane

   B on horseback

   C in covered wagons

   D by car

2 The United States wanted Americans to move to the Oregon Territory. Which reason best explains why?

   F The East was getting very crowded.

   G America wanted everyone to have their own farmland.

   H England wanted the Oregon Territory to belong to the United States.

   J To make Oregon part of America, more Americans than English had to live there.

3 All of the following reasons explain why people wanted to travel to the Oregon Territory EXCEPT

   A Everyone already had a covered wagon.

   B There was plenty of land for farming.

   C There was plenty of wildlife for hunting and fishing.

   D Stories made Oregon seem like a wonderful place.

4 Which of the following items best fits in the diagram below?

   F top made of leather

   G frame made of steel

   H wooden board to sit on

   J front and back wheels the same size

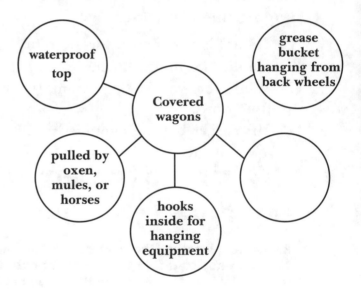

5 The Oregon Territory was made up of land that includes all of the following states EXCEPT?

   A California

   B Idaho

   C Washington

   D Oregon

Go On

How well did you do on these test questions? Check your answers.

1 How did most families travel to the West in the 1840s and 1850s?

A **Incorrect** Airplanes did not exist then.

B **Incorrect** Individuals might travel by horseback. But if you were with your family, most likely you used a covered wagon.

C **Correct** This is the way you would travel.

D **Incorrect** Cars did not exist then.

2 The United States wanted Americans to move to the Oregon Territory. Which reason best explains why?

F **Incorrect** The article does not mention the East being crowded.

G **Incorrect** This is not the reason the *government* wanted people to move there.

H **Incorrect** England wanted the Oregon Territory to belong to England.

J **Correct** America and England agreed that Oregon would belong to the country that could get more of its people living there.

3 All of the following reasons explain why people wanted to travel to the Oregon Territory EXCEPT

A **Correct** Everyone did not have a covered wagon. This is NOT a reason why they wanted to travel to the Oregon Territory.

B **Incorrect** People DID want to go there because there was plenty of land for farming.

C **Incorrect** People DID want to go there because there was plenty of wildlife for hunting and fishing.

D **Incorrect** People DID want to go there because stories made Oregon seem like a wonderful place.

4 Which of the following items best fits in the diagram below?

F **Incorrect** The top was made of canvas.

G **Incorrect** The frame was made of wood.

H **Correct** There was a wooden board to sit on.

J **Incorrect** The front wheels were smaller than the back wheels.

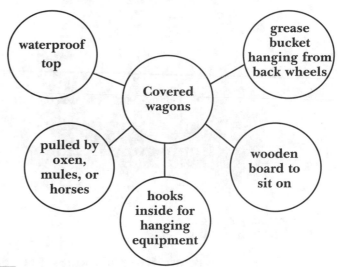

5 The Oregon Territory is made up of land that includes all of the following states EXCEPT?

A **Correct** The land that is now California was NOT part of it.

B **Incorrect** The land that is now Idaho was part of it.

C **Incorrect** The land that is now Washington was part of it.

D **Incorrect** The land that is now Oregon was part of it.

Remember This!

· · · · · · · · · · · ·

Finding main ideas and supporting details will help you be successful when reading informational text.

Writing is always about something. For example, a passage may be about cats. What the passage is about is called the *topic*.

When writers write, they often set out to tell you something. The most important idea a writer tells you about a topic is called the *main idea*. For example, the main idea of a passage may be that cats make great pets.

The writer makes the main idea even stronger by backing it up with details. These details—facts, figures, examples—are called *supporting details*. For example, a writer might back up the main idea that cats make great pets with these details.

Main Idea:	Cats make great pets.
Supporting Detail:	Cats like to sleep in your lap.
Supporting Detail:	It's fun to watch cats play.
Supporting Detail:	Cats make you feel good when they purr.

ACTIVITY

Directions **Here are five main ideas. For each main idea, write four details that support it.**

1.   **Main Idea:** There are many fun things for kids to do at the beach or shore.

Detail _____

Detail _____

Detail _____

Detail _____

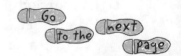

2.   **Main Idea:** Old photographs can tell you a lot about the past.

Detail _____

Detail _____

Detail _____

Detail _____

3.   **Main Idea:** Having a pet is a big responsibility.

Detail _____

Detail _____

Detail _____

Detail _____

4.   **Main Idea:** Fall is a season of bright colors.

Detail _____

Detail _____

Detail _____

Detail _____

5.   **Main Idea:** Ice cream comes in many flavors.

Detail _____

Detail _____

Detail _____

Detail _____

LESSON 5   Conclusions

ACTIVITY

Directions Read the paragraph below. Then answer the questions.

Airplane history comes alive when you visit the Aerodome in Rhinebeck, New York. The golden age of biplanes, or planes with two wings, comes to life right before your eyes. You can see the oldest flying plane in the United States. This plane was built in 1909. The most famous plane on display is actually a triplane, a plane with three wings. It was flown by the Red Baron in World War I. At air shows, these early planes actually take off and fly. Sometimes they even have fake air fights in the sky. If you want to see what early flight was like, the Aerodome is a good place to visit.

1. Write the statement that tells you the main idea of the paragraph above.

_____

_____

2. What is the first detail the author includes to support this main idea?

_____

_____

3. What is the second detail?

_____

_____

4. What is the third detail?

_____

_____

5. Write the conclusion–the statement that states again the main idea.

_____

_____

   Measuring Up™ to the New York State Learning Standards

LESSON 6   Apply to the Test

You've learned a lot about main ideas, supporting details, and conclusions. Here are samples of test questions dealing with these skills.

*D*irections
Read the passage from "Puffins, Clowns of the Sea." Then do Numbers 1-5.

from Puffins, Clowns of the Sea
Ruth J. Luhrs

Puffins live most of their lives on the open sea. They come ashore for only a few months each year to nest. Young birds not ready to mate may spend three years on the water before coming back to land. They're able to stay out so long because they can drink salt water and get rid of the salt through their nostrils.

Puffins are about the size of fat pigeons, with black backs and white bellies. Their large beaks are bright orange and yellow. They stand upright on land, like tiny penguins. In the water they look like ducks, with short, stiff black tail feathers fanning up to show white rears. Their big orange feet paddle like windup toys.

Some people call puffins sea clowns. During the spring nesting season, they grow blue patches on their beaks and near their eyes. Their faces are chalk white, and their eye markings make them look sad. They sway from side to side as they waddle along on gumboot feet. They fly like crazy bumblebees, looking as if they'll crash at any moment.

They're klutzy at flying and walking, but puffins are expert swimmers. They dive deep in search of food, using their strong wings like fins. They easily catch and swallow small fish.

Go On

Sample Main Idea Questions

1   **Which statement best expresses the main idea of the first paragraph?**

(A)   Puffins come ashore for a few months to nest.

B   Puffins can drink salt water.

C   Puffins live most of their lives on the open sea.

D   Young puffins may spend three years on the open water.

2   **Which of the following would be a good title for the second paragraph?**

F   A Bird to Make You Laugh

G   Puffins, Pigeons, and Penguins

(H)   A Bird That Looks Like a Duck

J   A Bird That Looks Like a Windup Toy

Sample Supporting Details Questions

3   **Which of the following items supports the idea that some people call puffins sea clowns?**

A   They have chalk white faces with big sad eyes.

B   They waddle along on gumboot feet.

C   When they fly, they look like crazy bumblebees.

(D)   All of the above.

4   **Which detail tells you something they are good at?**

F   walking

(G)   swimming

H   flying

J   none of the above

Sample Conclusion Question

5   **Which of the following statements would make a strong conclusion to this entire passage?**

A   Some people refer to puffins as "little brother of the north."

(B)   With their funny appearance and silly walk, puffins are sure to put a smile on your face.

C   Puffins are my favorite birds.

D   That's why puffins are known as good fishers.

LESSON 7 Independent Practice

Directions Have you ever wondered how the teddy bear was created? You'll find out as you read "Teddy's Bear." Then do Numbers 1-5 on the next page.

Teddy's Bear
Janeen R. Adil

Theodore "Teddy" Roosevelt, America's twenty-sixth president, was famous for accomplishing many important things while he was in office. Something he didn't do, however, made him just as famous. And because of it, one of the best-loved toys ever created was named after him.

In November 1902, President Roosevelt traveled south to settle a boundary dispute between Mississippi and Louisiana. While he was there, he took some time off to go bear hunting. Several reporters and a well-known newspaper artist named Clifford Berryman joined the president's hunting trip.

The hunters didn't have much luck. Finally, on the last day of the hunt, the president spotted a bear. As he carefully aimed his rifle, the animal turned around. It was only a cub! Teddy Roosevelt loved to hunt, but he refused to shoot the frightened little bear.

Clifford Berryman thought this was a wonderful opportunity for a drawing. He sketched a cartoon of President Roosevelt turning his back on the cub, unwilling to shoot the small creature. Soon Berryman's black-and-white drawing was appearing in newspapers all over the country. People everywhere liked the cartoon and thought it showed the president to be a kind-hearted man.

One of those who saw and enjoyed the drawing was Morris Michtom, a candy store owner in Brooklyn, New York. He and his wife, Rose, knew how to make stuffed toys, and the cartoon gave them an idea. The Michtoms found some brown plush fabric and cut out pieces for a bear with movable arms and legs. Then they sewed and stuffed the bear and added buttons for its eyes.

The Michtoms placed the new toy bear, a copy of Berryman's cartoon, and a sign that read "Teddy's Bear" in the front window of their store. The bear sold quickly, and so did the next few that the Michtoms made. When Morris saw how popular the bears were, he knew he would need the president's permission to continue using his name.

Go On

Morris wrote a letter to the White House and received a handwritten reply from Theodore Roosevelt himself. "I don't think my name is likely to be worth much in the bear business," the president wrote, "but you are welcome to use it." So the Michtoms went to work, making one teddy bear after another.

Since Rose and Morris made the bears themselves and still had a candy store to manage, they produced the bears slowly at first. Eventually they closed the candy store, and the Michtom family business became the Ideal Toy Company, one of America's biggest toy makers. Soon other companies in the United States and Europe were producing bears of all shapes, sizes, and prices. Some of the most beautiful stuffed bears were made in Germany by Margarete Steiff and her workers.

In just a few years, teddy bears had become extremely popular. Other items related to the stuffed bears were sold, too. Not only could one buy clothing for a teddy bear, but there were also bear puzzles, bear books, bear games, bear banks—all sorts of toys and amusements! Teddy bears had become as important to children as blocks, dolls, and balls had been for generations.

Today teddy bears remain a favorite of boys and girls everywhere. Many adults love to collect and display them, too. Hundreds of millions of teddy bears have been produced since Teddy Roosevelt's hunting trip so many years ago. Who could have guessed that the story of an unlucky president and a frightened bear cub would have such a happy ending?

Go On

Measuring Up™ to the New York State Learning Standards

1 **Which statement best states the main idea?**

A Teddy Roosevelt loved to hunt.

B One of America's best loved toys was named after Teddy Roosevelt.

C Rose and Morris Michtom started one of America's largest toy companies.

D People everywhere liked the cartoon of Teddy Roosevelt and the bear.

2 **Clifford Berryman was**

F a newspaper artist

G a toy maker

H a candy store owner

J none of the above

3 **Which of the following details supports the idea of how the teddy bear received its name?**

A The toy was made of brown plush fabric.

B Teddy is a cute name, just like the bear cub.

C The toy sold quickly, because people liked the name.

D The Michtoms put the toy bear in their store window next to the cartoon.

4 **Why did the Michtoms close their candy store?**

F The candy store wasn't making very much money.

G They wanted to devote their time to making teddy bears.

H Teddy Roosevelt ordered them to close down.

J German toy makers were making the stuffed bears.

5 **Which detail supports the conclusion that teddy bears remain a favorite of people everywhere?**

A Children today have other types of toys to play with.

B Hundreds of millions have been produced.

C Teddy Roosevelt's hunting trip had a happy ending.

D No one buys teddy bears any more.

Remember This!

Maps are great for finding out about places. A map is a detailed plan of a particular area. It may show different places–cities, towns, counties, regions. It may show different physical features–lakes, rivers, mountains. It usually indicates direction. Look at the map on the right.

Graphs help you picture the relation between numbers. A graph is a particular kind of chart. For example, the graph on the next page compares the height of Niagara Falls and Yellowstone Falls. The chart below it provides the same information.

NIAGARA FALLS

Whirlpool

UNITED STATES

CANADA

Lower Niagara River

Gorge

N

SCALE IN MILES
0   .5   1

Prospect Point
American Falls
Bridal Veil Falls
Terrapin Rock
Horseshoe Falls
Goat Island
Hermit's Cascade
Three Sisters Islands
(Asenath, Angeline, Celinda Eliza)
Niagara River
Rapids

ACTIVITY

Directions Use the map to the right to answer these questions.

1. What are the names of the Three Sister Islands?

_____

2. If you traveled from Bridal Veil Falls to Prospect Point, in what direction would you be traveling?

_____

3. What river flows into the Falls?

_____

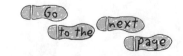
Go to the next page

Bar Graph

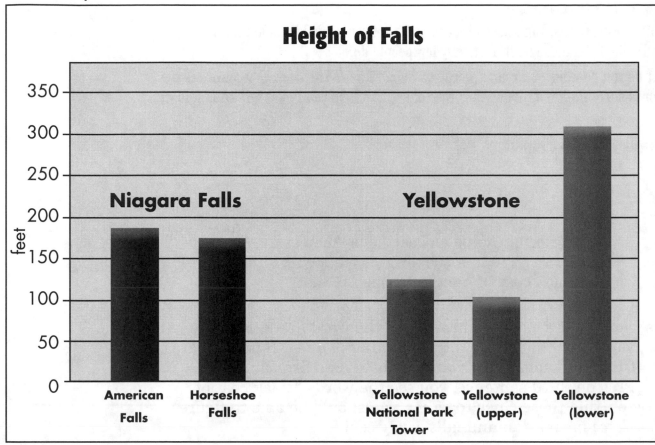

ACTIVITY

Directions Use the graph and chart to answer these questions.

4. Which falls has the highest height, or elevation?

_____

5. How much higher are the American Falls than the Horseshoe Falls?

_____

Chart

Height of Falls	
NIAGARA FALLS	
American Falls	182 ft
Horseshoe Falls	173 ft
YELLOWSTONE	
Yellowstone National Park Tower	132 ft
Yellowstone (upper)	109 ft
Yellowstone (lower)	308 ft

LESSON 9   Context

Remember This!

• • • • • • • • • • • • • • •

Words, words, words. You know a lot of words, but you probably do not know every word in the English language. In fact, very few people do.

What do you do when you read a word you do not know? The *context* of a word is the other words surrounding it. Sometimes the context can help you figure out an unknown word.

Look at the sentences below.

Example

> The *fleece* of the polar bear helps keep it warm. Why? When the air gets trapped inside the thick coat of hair, it warms up.

Suppose you don't know the meaning of the word *fleece*. From the context, you know that fleece has something to do with polar bears. In fact, it is what keeps them warm. This is your first clue to the meaning. In the third sentence, you see the words "thick coat of hair." By putting these clues together, you should be able to figure out that *fleece* means "an animal's wooly coat."

ACTIVITY

Directions **Now try it on your own. In the sentences below, use context to figure out the meaning of each *italicized* word. Write your definition on the line after each sentence.**

1. The label said that the blanket was *flammable*. Luis knew that he had to keep something that could catch fire away from the baby.

   It can get on fire easily

2. The bike needs oil. The gears are squeaking. You should *lubricate* them so that they work more smoothly.

   put oil on them

3. He felt nervous and afraid. He had serious *qualms* about going on the roller coaster.

fear

4. The video showed how the earth began to *quake*. As the earth shook and trembled, the house began to fall.

shake

5. The king was losing his *domination* over the colonies. The more the colonists spoke up, the more control he lost.

control

6. When we visited Hawaii, we saw a *dormant* volcano. It had not shown any signs of action for hundreds of years.

not exploding

7. The pirate knew the mate would *double-cross* him. He waited for the moment the mate would show he was not loyal.

against

8. They searched for *fossils* along the riverbank. They found several rocks that showed traces of animals and plants from ages ago.

animal bonesfrom along time ago

9. "The price is *outrageous*," Amanda said. "I can go next door and buy the same thing for half as much."

great   crazy

10. The nurse tried to improve *sanitary* conditions. Keeping the homes clean and free of germs was his goal.

cleaness

LESSON 10   Apply to the Test

Y ou've learned a lot about reading maps, graphs, and charts and about using context clues. Here are samples of test questions dealing with these skills.

Directions

Read the passage from "Welcome to the Rain Forest." Then do Numbers 1-5.

Welcome to the Rain Forest
Karen E. Hong

More than 500 years ago, Christopher Columbus provided the world with the first known written description of a rain forest. "I never saw a lovelier sight," he wrote, "trees everywhere, lining the river, green and beautiful. They are not like our own, and each has its own flowers and fruit. Many birds, large and small, singing sweetly away."

For the next 400 years, people called these areas by familiar terms: forest or jungle. Then, in 1898, A.F.W. Schimper, a German botanist (a person who studies plants), gave these unusual areas a special name–*tropische Regenwald* (tropical rain forest.).

Two characteristics separate the tropical rain forest from other forests: temperature and rainfall. Equatorial rain forests exist where the rainfall is high (160 to 400 inches per year) and the average temperature is high (80°F). Here there are no cold or dry spells. Tropical moist forests receive less rain (40 to 160 inches per year). Their temperature is not as constant, and they have a dry season when some of the trees lose their leaves.

Two thirds of today's existing rain forests are equatorial; that is, they lie near or on the equator. More than half of these border the Amazon River in South America. In fact, six percent of the world's rain forests are located in Peru.

	RAIN FOREST	MOIST FOREST
YEARLY RAINFALL	160-400 inches	40-160 inches
AVERAGE TEMPERATURE	80°F	changes

★ capital city
- - - international border
—— rivers
- - - equator

28 English Language Arts • Level D
Copying is illegal.
Measuring Up™ to the New York State Learning Standards

LESSON 10   Apply to the Test

Sample Questions About Maps,
Graphs, and Charts

1 The Amazon River passes through which country?

A Bolivia
B Argentina
C Peru
D Columbia

2 The capital of Peru is

F Buenos Aires
G Lima
H Santiago
J none of the above

3 The lowest amount of rain per year in a rain forest is

A 160 inches
B 400 inches
C 40 inches
D 60 inches

Sample Context Questions

4 A botanist is

F a scientist who studies plants
G a scientist who studies animals
H a doctor who treats people in rain forests
J a scientist who studies bones

5 The word *equatorial* means

A in the country of Ecuador
B a rain forest
C lying near or on the equator
D none of the above

Directions The following article tells about doing research on the Internet. Read the article. Then do Numbers 1-5 on the next page.

The Internet
Deborah Heiligman

An interesting place to do research is the Internet. The Internet is a network of computers all over the world. Many computers in libraries, schools, and homes are set up to use the Internet. If you can't connect from home or school, ask your public librarian if you can do Internet research at the library.

Give yourself plenty of time to use the Internet. Plan in advance. First, you might have to make an appointment at school or at the public library to use it. Second, it may take you a while to find what you're looking for. Even experienced Internet users hit dead ends on-line. If you're new at it, you can expect to hit even more. But don't let this discourage you. There's a lot of information in cyberspace that would be useful for your report.

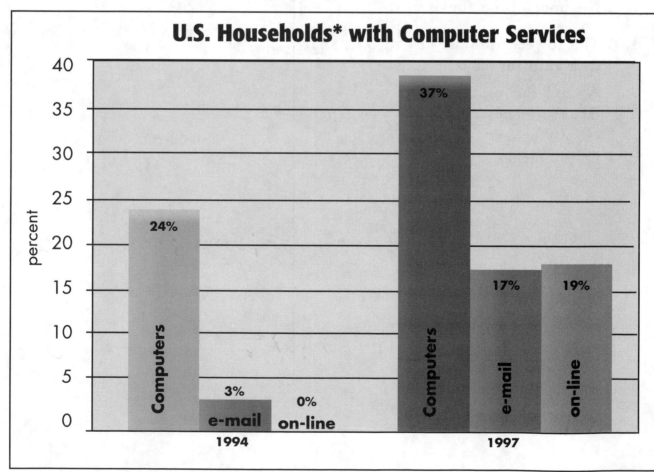

U.S. Households* with Computer Services

1994: Computers 24%, e-mail 3%, on-line 0%
1997: Computers 37%, e-mail 17%, on-line 19%

Source: U.S. Department of Commerce
*household: All the people who live together in a house or apartment

Go On

Check out Internet guides. This article will get you started doing research in cyberspace. But you should also take a look at Internet guides for kids. There are new ones coming out all the time. Ask your librarian or bookseller to recommend some good ones.

There are also Internet yellow pages and directories (for kids and adults) that can help you find Web sites, newsgroups, magazines, and other information on the Internet.

A Web site is a group of pages on the World Wide Web, the part of the Internet that has pictures, sound, and video as well as text. A Web site may be put together by a person (an author, for example); a group (a fifth-grade class); an organization (the Chocolate Manufacturers Association); an institution (The New York Public Library); a museum (The British Museum); a government agency (NASA); or a state, city, or town.

When you are doing research on the Web, it is good to go to the Web site put together by an organization or institution, rather than by an individual. Those Web sites are usually more detailed, and the information is more likely to be accurate. Using the Internet can be a frustrating experience—an experience of going from poor Web site to poor Web site. But when you hit gold, it's terrific.

Go On

1   All of the following statements tell how the Internet is like a library EXCEPT

A   You can find many sources of information.

B   You need to use a computer to find the information.

C   You can browse, or look around casually for information.

D   It's a good place to do research.

2   You want to go on the Internet to do research. What is the best thing to do if you don't have a computer at home or school?

F   Ask your public librarian if you can do Internet research at the library.

G   Wait until you get a computer.

H   Read the Internet yellow pages.

J   Ask someone who has a computer to do the research for you.

3   The author's main purpose, or reason, for writing this article is

A   to entertain you.

B   to show how much she knows.

C   to provide information.

D   to get you to buy the Internet yellow pages.

4   Think about the information in the graph on page 30. Which statement is correct?

F   In 1997, more households had e-mail than computers.

G   Almost 20% of households had on-line services in 1997.

H   Almost 40% of households had computers in 1994.

J   Almost 40% of households had e-mail in 1994.

5   Why is it a good idea to go to a Web site put together by an organization instead of an individual?

A   You are likely to get personal opinions.

B   The information is likely to be more detailed and accurate.

C   You might know the person who put together the Web site.

D   Only organizations can give you accurate information.

ACTIVITIES

 Reading

One question to ask yourself when you read is "Who is this written for?" For example, something might be written for a kindergarten student, a fourth grader, or an adult. The group of people something is written for is called the *audience*.

Visit your public library. Find a book about insects written for kindergarten students. Find another book about insects written with students your age in mind. How are these books different? Look at the illustrations. Look at the language. Look at how much information they have. Jot down your findings on the lines below. Then share what you find with your classmates.

_____

_____

_____

_____

_____

 Listening

Many newscasts provide information by answering the questions Who? What? Where? When? Why? and How? Listen to a newscast on television or radio. Jot down answers to these questions.

Who?_____

What?_____

When?_____

Where?_____

Why?_____

How?_____

ACTIVITIES

 Writing

Suppose you need to find information for a report about the Finger Lakes in New York State. Jot down the steps you would take to find this information. Number the steps first, second, third, and so on.

_____

_____

_____

_____

_____

_____

_____

Speaking

Work with a small group. Have each person in your group talk to two adults to find information about the history of your community. Have a panel discussion, sharing what you have found with your classmates. Be prepared to answer questions from the audience.

Write your notes here.

_____

_____

_____

_____

_____

_____

_____

_____

Measuring Up™ to the New York State Learning Standards

Chapter 2 IMAGINATIVE LITERATURE

What's It All About?

In this chapter, you will learn

✸ what imaginative literature is

✸ strategies for reading imaginative literature

✸ how to answer multiple choice questions

✸ how to understand sequence of events

✸ how to make inferences about characters

✸ how to understand plot and theme

✸ how to use punctuation to read poetry

Do these situations sound familiar?

1. You are at a Halloween party. You and your friends try to scare each other by telling ghost stories.

2. It's a beautiful summer evening. Your family takes you to a performance of a play in the park.

3. It's a cold winter night. You curl up in bed with a good novel.

4. It's summertime and your family is driving to the mountains. You listen to an audiocassette of your favorite novel.

Go to the next page

Imaginative Literature Is All Around You!

Visit a bookstore. Learn the pleasure of browsing, or looking around without any particular purpose. You're sure to encounter a novel or book of poems you want to read. Have you met Wolfgang Amadeus Mouse, for example? You'll encounter him in Dick King-Smith's *A Mouse Called Wolf*. Have you giggled at the fun poems of Shel Silverstein? A good collection of his poetry is *Falling Up*. Have you spent time with Mayo Cornelius Higgins? You'll get to know him in *M. C. Higgins, the Great* by Virginia Hamilton.

New York State offers many special opportunities. You can see plays performed at theaters throughout the state. Museums such as the *Museum of Television and Radio* in New York City offer unique opportunities. Here you can view programs about the making of animated features or look at early television shows. Homes of famous writers offer even more chances to see literature come to life. At *Sunnyside*, the home of Washington Irving in Tarrytown, you can see "The Legend of Sleepy Hollow" performed. At the Mark Twain Study and Exhibit in Elmira, New York, you can learn more about this great writer.

 ## ACTIVITY

Directions Work with a partner or a parent. Fill out the chart below. List at least four places to read, perform, listen to, or view literature.

Literature Is All Around Us
1.
2.
3.
4.

LESSON 1 What Is Imaginative Literature?

Imaginative literature springs from the writer's mind. It is different from nonfiction. Nonfiction tells about true events or provides facts about a subject. Fiction is made-up. It tells you about characters and events that are not real. The people, or characters, in the story, did not really live. The events did not really happen.

Realistic and Fantastic Literature

Some imaginative literature may be *realistic*. This means that the characters *seem* like people in real life. The things that happen to them *seem* like things that happen to real people. But the characters never really existed. The events never really happened. They are imaginary. *Sarah, Plain and Tall* by Patricia MacLachlan is a good example of a realistic story.

Some of the literature may be *fantastic*. This means that the characters may be somewhat strange and unbelievable. The events are not likely to happen in real life. For example, a three-headed talking spider might be a character in a fantastic story. The setting—or time and place—may be fantastic. For example, the story may take place on another planet or in the future. *Peter Pan* is a good example of a fantastic story.

We all like a good story and imaginative literature is fun to read. Imaginative literature also helps us understand life. When we read a good story, we connect with it. We connect the characters and what happens to them to people we know and things that happen in our own lives.

Go to the next page

Types of Imaginative Literature

Novels	A novel is a long work of fiction that tells about made-up people and events. Some novels are divided into chapters, or smaller units. You've probably read many novels already. For example, you may have read *A Million Fish. . .More or Less* by Patricia C. McKissack.
Short Stories	Like its name says, a short story is a short work of literature. Usually it can be read in a brief period of time. You often find short stories in magazines. They also come in collections, such as *The Short Stories of Mark Twain*.
Myths, Legends, and Folktales	Myths, legends, and folktales are stories handed down from earlier times. Myths often tell about the gods and goddesses of a group of people. For example, you have probably read and heard myths about Hercules and his dealings with other gods and goddesses of ancient Greece. Legends and folktales often give colorful explanations for natural events. Many contain animal characters. For example, you may have read African tales telling about Anansi the Spider.
Plays	A play is a story that is acted out, or performed, usually in a theater or on a stage. Actors take the parts of the characters. You may also see a play on television or you may hear a play on the radio. Sometimes you can read a play in a magazine or book.
Poetry	A poem is writing set down in lines. Often poems have rhythm, or a set beat. Rhythm gives the poem its musical quality. Sometimes the words at the end of lines rhyme. Songs are a type of poem. Think of them as poetry set to music. Poems often create vivid word pictures.
Electronic Books	Imaginative literature is available on CD-ROM. CD-ROMs allow you to interact with the stories. On some, you can make the characters move. You can find definitions of words you do not know. You can find information about the author.

Go to the next page

LESSON 1 What is Imaginative Literature?

ACTIVITY

Directions Create a personal list of hits. Pick three of your all-time favorites. Write the title and author. Then write three to four lines telling what the story is about. Be ready to tell your classmates why you chose each story.

1 Title _____

Author _____

Summary _____

_____

_____

_____

2 Title _____

Author _____

Summary _____

_____

_____

_____

3 Title _____

Author _____

Summary _____

_____

_____

_____

LESSON 2 How to Read Imaginative Literature

You have practiced reading informational text and answering multiple choice questions. Now you are going to develop even more strategies that will help you read imaginative text with greater understanding.

Keys to Success

These strategies will help you be successful when reading imaginative literature. On page 42, you will see how to put these strategies to work.

When you read, look for

Sequence of Events

Sequence of events is the order of the events in a story. First one thing happens. Then something else happens. Then a third event happens, and so on. When you read, make sure you understand the order of events.

Writers often tell events in time order. In other words, they tell what happens first, then second, then third, and finally last. Sometimes, though, they mix up the order of events. They start with what happened last to make you curious. Then they tell you the events that led up to this final situation.

Plot

When you tell what happens in a story, you are telling its plot. The plot is the plan for what happens in the story. Usually the main character faces a problem. The story ends when the problem is solved.

Inferences About Characters

The characters are the people in the story. For example, Pippi and Tommy and Annika are all characters in the novel *Pippi Longstocking* by Astrid Lindgren. Sometimes these characters are actually animals. For example, Charlotte is the unforgettable spider in E. B. White's *Charlotte's Web*.

An *inference* is an intelligent guess you make after looking at all the details. When you read, you make inferences about the characters. You use details from what they say and what they do to decide what they are like. For example, you might decide that a character that people think is mean is really kind. You base your inference on details from the story.

Go to the next page

Theme

The theme is the story's meaning. It is the insight into life revealed through the story. For example, when you read a story about a girl fighting for survival in the wilderness, you might enjoy it because it's a good adventure yarn. You also might come to understand something special about life. Through the girl's experiences, you see that fear is something all people experience, but fear can be conquered. This insight is the story's theme.

Punctuation That Helps You Read Poetry

Poetry is written in lines. A line of poetry does not necessarily signal the end of a sentence. When you read poetry, look for punctuation marks that signal the end of a sentence. These end marks are periods (.), question marks (?), and exclamation points (!).

READING GUIDE

Directions Put it all together. Use all the strategies you have learned so far to help you read "The Hungry Goddess." The questions and comments on the side will help improve your comprehension of this Aztec myth.

❶The Hungry Goddess
❷An Aztec Myth
❸*Retold by Olga Loya*

❹ Once long ago the Aztec gods lived high up. In those days there was no sky and no earth. There was only water and water and water. There was water from nowhere to nowhere.

❺ Among the gods there was a goddess. She was called La Diosa Hambrienta, the Hungry Goddess, because she had eyes and mouths all over her body. She had them on her face, her chest, her stomach and her legs and arms. She had mouths and eyes at her elbows, wrists, ankles, waist—everywhere. She was always hungrily trying to see what was happening. She was always trying to eat, and she was always crying out,

"Tengo hambre, tengo hambre—I am hungry."
All day long she would wail, "Tengo hambre."
All night long she would say, "Tengo hambre."
Day in and day out, she called out, "Tengo hambre."

❻ Finally all the gods went to the most powerful gods of all and said, "Por favor, can't you do something?" The woman is always crying. We can't think. We can't sleep. She's always saying, "Tengo hambre."

Now the two most powerful gods were Quetzalcoatl and Tezcatlipoca. The gods called Quetzalcoatl the Plumed Serpent because he wore such beautifully flowing feathers of many colors and he walked with a stick carved in the shape of a serpent. He dressed in white. He wore gold hoop earrings, bells around his legs, and pearls on his sandals. He also wore a mask shaped like a bird's head called the Wind Mask. With that mask, he could blow the wind for a long distance. Thus he was known as the Wind God and the God of Light.

● GUIDED QUESTIONS

❶ The title raises a *question*. Why is the goddess hungry? Read on to find out.

❷ Do you know who the Aztecs are? Stop to *clarify*. The Aztecs are the native people who lived in Mexico. They built a great civilization before the Spanish came to the New World.

❸ Notice the word *retold. Myths* are stories passed down from generation to generation. Who is the storyteller?

❹ What is unusual about the setting of this story? Is it *realistic* or *fantastic*?

❺ The words *Diosa Hambrienta* are Spanish. The context tells you the meaning of these words. What do you think *diosa hambrienta* means?

❻ Why do the gods go to the most powerful gods of all? What *inference* can you make about how they feel?

READING GUIDE

7 Tezcatlipoca dressed in black. He wore rattlesnake rattles around his legs. He was sometimes called the God **8** of Smoking Mirror because he wore an *obsidian* mirror made of black volcanic glass on his foot, with which he could see everything that was happening in the world. Tezcatlipoca's other name was the God of Darkness.

9 Quetzalcoatl and Tezcatlopoca talked and talked. Finally they decided they would take La Diosa Hambrienta to the water; maybe the water would calm her. So they flew down to the water to see if there was anything there for the goddess to eat. Quetzalcoalt blew with his Wind Mask. He blew and blew, and the water went this way and that. They could find nothing at all.

● GUIDED QUESTIONS

7 Compare and contrast the appearance of Quetzalcoatl (ket säl′kōt əl) and Tezcatlipoca (tet kät′lə po′kəl). Why is one called the God of Light and the other the God of Darkness?

8 *Context* tells you the meaning of the word *obsidian*. What does this word mean?

9 Look at the *sequence of events*. What did Quetzalcoatl and Tezcatlipoca do before they took the hungry goddess to the water? Why did they do this?

They flew up to La Diosa Hambrienta and carried her down to the water. On the way down, she continued to cry, "Tengo hambre. Tengo hambre."

They put her on the water. She was silent. She was floating so quietly, so calmly.

The gods said, "Ah, she is now happy."

But no, she started to cry out again: "Tengo hambre. Tengo hambre."

Quetzalcoatl and Tezcatlipoca were very upset. They transformed themselves into huge serpents and took hold of La Diosa Hambrienta. One god took her right hand and left foot and the other her left hand and right foot. They started to pull and pull. But the goddess was very strong. She fought them long and hard. It was the most difficult fight the gods had ever fought. As they continued to struggle, they accidentally snapped her in half.

❿ Quetzalcoatl and Tezcatlipoca were very surprised and very sorry. They took the bottom half--from the waist to the feet—of La Diosa Hambrienta to the other gods and said, "Look what we have done!"

"What a shame," the other gods said. "Wait, we will use this half of the hungry woman and it shall be the sky."

The gods looked at the goddess's top half. "Poor thing," they said. "Look how unhappy she is. What can we do? Let us make her happy."

⓫ So they transformed her hair into the forests. Her skin became the lakes, the rivers and the ocean. Her mouth became the caves; shoulders became the mountains. She became Mother Earth—the Earth we live on to this day.

All the gods said, "Ah, now she will be happy!"

But no! She again started to wail, "Tengo hambre. Tengo hambre."

To this day, La Diosa Hambrienta, Mother Earth, is still hungry and thirsty. When it rains, she swallows all the water. If a tree falls and dies, she eats it. When a flower wilts and dies, she eats it. She is always hungry.

⓬ Sometimes when the wind is blowing late at night, if you listen very carefully, you might still hear her calling, "Tengo Haaambreee; tengo haaambree."

❿ **Notice how the two gods behave in this paragraph. What *inferences* do you make about them based on their behavior?**

⓫ **Details in this passage support the idea that the two gods were sorry for what they had done to the hungry goddess. Find two *details* that support this idea. Tell them in *order of sequence*.**

⓬ ***Myths, legends,* and *folktales* often provide colorful explanations of common events in nature. What events does this myth seek to explain?**

Prepare for the Test

The New York State Language Arts test is a timed test. On the first day of the test, you have to finish all your work in 45 minutes. You have to read the passages and answer the multiple choice questions in this time period. At the end of 45 minutes, you will be told to put your pencil down.

Planning your time is important to doing well on the test. The following strategies will help you plan your time well.

Test Taking Strategies

Read All Questions First

After you read each passage, read through all of the multiple choice questions that go with it before you start to answer them. This will give you a good picture of what the questions are about. It will also give you time to get your mind warmed up.

Easiest First

Start by answering the easiest multiple choice questions. These are the questions you are sure you know the answers to. Then go back and answer the more difficult questions.

Keep Track of Time

Don't spend too much time on one item. If you are having difficulty with a question, skip it. Then come back to the question later.

Answer Every Question

Remember to go back to those skipped questions. You will get no credit if you don't answer a question. Start by taking out the choice that seems wrong. Then whittle the choices down until you have only one or two possible answers. If necessary, guess.

Double-check

Double-check your answer. Say the answer to yourself. Does it sound right? Ask yourself if your answer makes sense.

Match Your Answer to the Correct Letter

A simple mistake is filling in the wrong letter. You know the answer is B but you fill in C by mistake. Don't lose credit because you made a careless error.

SAMPLE TEST

Multiple Choice Questions

*D*irections
Try your hand at answering these multiple choice questions. They tell how well you understood the myth "The Hungry Goddess."

1 Which of the following titles best fits this myth?

A Quetzalcoatl and Tezcatlipoca
B Why Mother Earth is Hungry
C Gods and Goddesses of the Aztec
D Solving the Problem of World Hunger

2 The following diagram shows how Quetzalcoatl and Tezcatlipoca are different. Which item below best fits in the overlapping circles? This detail shows how they are alike.

F Could change into a serpent
G Had a mask shaped like a bird's head
H Was called the Plumed Serpent
J Walked with a stick carved in the shape of a serpent

Wore bells on legs
God of Light
Had pearls in sandals
Dressed in white

Wore rattlesnake rattles on legs
God of Darkness
Had mirror on foot
Dressed in black

3 After they took the hungry goddess down to the water, why did Quetzalcoatl blow on his Wind Mask?

A He wanted the hungry goddess to float quietly on the water.
B He liked the way it felt to blow on the mask.
C Tezcatlipoca didn't have a Wind Mask.
D He wanted to find food for the goddess.

4 Which of the following events happened FIRST?

F Quetzalcoatl and Tezcatlipoca turned themselves into serpents.
G Quetzalcoatl and Tezcatlipoca pulled the goddess apart.
H Half of the hungry goddess's body became the sky.
J The gods asked Quetzalcoatl and Tezcatipoca for a favor.

5 Which of the following is NOT a fantastic detail?

A The hungry goddess has eyes and mouths all over her body.
B Quetzalcoatl and Tezcatlipoca change into serpents.
C You can hear the wind blowing at night.
D The eyes of the hungry goddess became lakes.

Go On

How well did you do on these questions?

1 **Which of the following titles best fits this myth?**

A **Incorrect** This myth is mostly about the Hungry Goddess, not the two gods.

B **Correct** This is a good title since the myth explains why Mother Earth is always hungry.

C **Incorrect** This title is too broad. The myth does not tell you about all the gods and goddesses.

D **Incorrect** The myth has nothing to do with solving the problem of world hunger.

2 **The following diagram shows how Quetzalcoatl and Tezcatlipoca are different. Which item below best fits in the overlapping circles? This detail shows how they are alike.**

F **Correct** Both gods could change into a serpent.

G **Incorrect** Only Quetzalcoatl had a mask shaped like a bird's head.

H **Incorrect** Only Quetzalcoatl was called the Plumed Serpent.

J **Incorrect** Only Quetzalcoatl walked with a stick carved in the shape of a serpent.

     Quetzalcoatl   **Tezcatlipoca**

Wore bells on legs
God of Light
Had pearls in sandals
Dressed in white

Could change into a serpent

Wore rattlesnake rattles on legs
God of Darkness
Had mirror on foot
Dressed in black

3 **After they took the hungry goddess down to the water, why did Quetzalcoatl blow on his Wind Mask?**

A **Incorrect** Blowing on his mask would stir up the water.

B **Incorrect** The myth does not tell us how he felt about blowing on the mask.

C **Incorrect** This fact is correct, but it doesn't answer the question.

D **Correct** When he blew on his Wind Mask, he could see whether there were any fish.

4 **Which of the following events happened FIRST?**

F **Incorrect** This event happened second. First the gods ask Quetzalcoatl and Tezcatlipoca for a favor. Then they turn themselves into serpents. Next they pull the goddess apart. After that, her eyes become lakes.

G **Incorrect** See the correct order.

H **Incorrect** See the correct order.

J **Correct** The order is J, F, G, H.

5 **Which of the following is NOT a fantastic detail?**

A **Incorrect** A goddess with eyes and mouths all over her body IS certainly unusual.

B **Incorrect** Two gods changing into serpents certainly IS unusual.

C **Correct** The fact that you can hear the wind blow at night is NOT fantastic.

D **Incorrect** Her eyes becoming lakes IS fantastic.

LESSON 4   Sequence of Events

Remember This!

• • • • • • • • • • • • • • •

Sequence of events is the order of events in the story. Another term for sequence of events is time order. When you read, keep track of what happens first, what happens second, what happens next, and so on. Some words help you keep track of the sequence of events.

First	Next	Later
Second	Following	After
Third	Before	Then
Last	Recently	

In the following paragraph, the words that help you see the sequence of events are printed in italics.

Kendra and Ricky were helping to build a community garden. *First* they planned a rummage sale to raise money. *Then*, with the money earned through the sale, they bought seeds and bulbs. The beautiful pictures on the packages filled them with dreams of how wonderful their garden would look once they were done. *Next* they planted the seeds and bulbs and watered the soil. *Later* that spring they were filled with delight as the first flowers peeked through the ground. But the most wonderful event happened *after* the flowers were in full bloom. A reporter from the local newspaper interviewed Kendra and Ricky about the garden. They couldn't help but smile *when* a picture of them standing in their garden appeared on the front page of the paper.

 Go to the next page

TIME OUT FOR SKILLS

ACTIVITY

Directions Read the opening sentence below. Then put the events that follow it in time order. Write 1 next to the event that happened first. Write 2 next to the event that happened second. Write 3 next to the event that happened third. Write 4 next to the event that happened fourth. Write 5 next to the event that happened last.

"The land where City Hall now stands has an interesting history," said Mr. Ruiz, as he walked the children around the building.

_____   Recently, New York City decided to fix up the land around City Hall.

_____   The Dutch settlers in New Amsterdam first used the land as a pasture.

_____   After work on the renovation began, imagine the surprise when workers found the remains of an African burial ground.

_____   Next the island came under British rule.

_____   The British used the land as the site of a poorhouse.

ACTIVITY

Directions Now try it on your own. Read the story starter below. Then write four events in time order.

"The Martians are landing! The Martians are landing!" shouted Wanda.

First _____

_____

Next _____

_____

Then _____

_____

Finally _____

_____

LESSON 5   Inferences About Characters

TIME OUT FOR SKILLS

Remember This!

• • • • • • • • • • • • •

Sometimes an author tells you exactly what a character is like.

Emilio was brave and courageous.

Sometimes the author shows you.

The battle blazed on. The guns blared. The cannons roared. Fear made his knees tremble. But still the soldier pushed on past enemy lines to save his friend.

In the passage above, the author never tells you that the soldier is brave. Look at the details—the guns blaring, the cannons roaring, the soldier pressing on to save his friend in spite of his fear. These details help you make the inference that the soldier is indeed courageous.

An inference is an intelligent guess you make based on evidence in the story. When you read about characters in a story, ask yourself questions like:

✱ What is this character really like?

✱ Why is she acting this way?

✱ How is he feeling?

✱ Why did she do that?

If the author doesn't tell you directly, as you read, find evidence in the story that helps you answer these questions.

Go to the next page

ACTIVITY

Directions Read each passage below. Write an inference
you would make about the character in each passage.

"I want the bandit brought to me now!" shouted the king.
He pounded his hand against the side of the throne. He
puffed up his chest. His face turned bright red. "Now!" he
demanded. His thunderous voice could be heard in the back of
the throne room. "Not tomorrow. Not the next day. If the
bandit is not brought to me by sunset, you shall not see another
sunrise."

1. What inference do you make about the king? _____

_____

_____

2. What evidence supports your answer?_____

_____

_____

Randi's birthday was just three days away. "Oh, what shall
I buy?" thought Lorraine, as she looked around the mall
with her mother.
    "A game?" asked Mom.
    "A game would be fun. But she has so many!"
    "A stuffed animal?"
    "Maybe a real animal would do it," replied Lorraine.
    As they stepped off the elevator leading to the pet store,
they ran right into Randi.
    "Oh, gosh!" said Lorraine. "I didn't expect to see you here."
And she turned bright red.

3. What inference do you make about how Lorraine is feeling? _____

_____

4. Why is she feeling this way? _____

_____

5. What evidence backs up your answer?_____

_____

You've learned a lot about following the sequence of events and making inferences about characters. Here are samples of test questions dealing with these skills.

Directions
Read this passage from "Just Hang in There!" Then do Numbers 1-5.

Just Hang in There!
Jim Janik

The big left-hander on the mound fired the baseball home.

"Hey!" Josh had only a fraction of a second to jerk his head out of the path of the speeding baseball. He flopped onto his back with a thud, the air kicking out from his lungs on impact.

"Strike one!" the umpire yelled.

The Mudcat catcher towered over Josh, holding the ball. "Nice curve, huh?" he chuckled, smirking down at him, then threw the baseball to his pitcher.

"You have to hang in there on that curve ball, Josh!" Coach Schmidt hollered from the third-base coach's box.

Josh, a left-handed hitter, was not used to seeing a left-hander's curve ball breaking away from him. All the right-handed pitchers in the league threw curve balls that curved toward him, right into his swing, right where he liked it.

Josh dusted off his uniform and eased back into the batter's box.

"Let's give him another curve. That kid's a big chicken!" the Mudcat catcher yelled to the grinning pitcher.

"Just hang in there," Josh told himself. The next pitch came whistling in just like the first, heading right at him. Every muscle in Josh's body screamed at him to get out of the way. He remembered how foolish he had felt jumping away from the first pitch before it broke sharply over the plate for a strike. He decided to hang in there.

But this time the pitch didn't break. It was a fastball. The ball crashed into Josh's shoulder, and he bent over, clutching at the pounding pain in his arm.

Josh slowly trotted down to first base, shaking his hand, trying to coax some feeling back into his arm.

When Josh came up to hit the next time, the catcher shouted out to the pitcher, "Let's put one in his ear this time."

Coach Schmidt called Josh over for a conference. "Remember to hold your ground on that curve ball. Don't let yourself bail out."

"But how can I tell if it's going to curve?" Josh asked.

"You'll learn. Just watch the seams."

"But what if I'm wrong," Josh thought. He stretched his stiff arm over his head. Sooner or later he would have to learn to hit the curve.

Sample Sequence of Events Questions

1 **Which of the following events happens first?**

A   The Mudcat pitcher calls Josh a chicken.

B   Josh jumps away from the speeding ball.

C   Josh flops onto his back.

D   The coach tells Josh to hang in there.

2 **Which of the following events happens last?**

F   Josh gets hit by a fastball.

G   The pitcher throws a curve ball.

H   The coach tells Josh not to let himself bail out.

J   Josh remembers what it was like to play against right-handed pitchers.

Sample Inference About Character Questions

3 **Which detail helps you infer that Josh is really quite brave?**

A   He jumps away from the ball.

B   He goes up to bat again, even though he had been hit.

C   He's a left-handed hitter.

D   He usually plays against right-handed pitchers.

4 **All of the following words describe Josh EXCEPT**

F   a coward

G   a left-hander

H   nervous

J   determined

5 **Which details makes you think that Josh is more confident when he plays against right-handed pitchers.**

A   He listens to the coach's advice.

B   When a right-hander throws a ball, it curves right into his swing.

C   Left-handed pitchers are better pitchers than right-handed ones.

D   The coach is a right-handed pitcher.

***D**irections*
"Pa's Wonderful Girl" is a realistic story. Read the short story. Then do Numbers 1-5 on the next page.

Pa's Wonderful Girl
Barbara Esposito

Addie coughed as she stuffed oiled rags between the window sashes. "Get them in tight," Ma said.

Outside, the wind raked gullies into their South Dakota farmland. Pa gulped down his coffee and shook his head. "Looks like another bad one coming."

"If this drought keeps up, our farm will blow away," Ma said. "Maybe we should just pack up and move on."

"Pa gave Ma a long look. "We're not quitters. When things get tough, we stick it through."

Bessie mooed from the barn. "Sounds like she agrees with you, Pa." Addie said.

"I'd better check on my sweet, wonderful girl." Pa pulled his neckerchief up around his face and went out.

Addie sighed. "Sometimes I think Pa loves that cow more than us."

Her mother frowned. "Addie! That's no way to talk. You know Bessie keeps us going. We depend on her for milk and cream."

Yes, Addie thought. Bessie's cream waited in the crock. Addie churned it while William played on the floor. When she finished, she put the butter on a plate, covered it, and set it on a shelf in the root cellar. By then, choking dust covered everything in the house. It rippled along the kitchen floor and swirled against the cellar door. The wind had picked up, too, turning the clouds into great rolling waves.

Ma opened the door a crack. "I've never seen anything this bad." She pushed the door shut. "Your pa should be back by now. Something must have happened. He wouldn't stay out in weather as bad as this." She turned to Addie. "I'll go look. Stay here and watch William."

Ma wrapped a shawl around her head. "Don't go out for anything. I'll be right back." She walked head down into the wind, struggling with each step. In a wink, Ma disappeared into the dark wall of dust.

Minutes passed. Addie grew uneasy. What had happened to Pa? Where was Ma now?

Go On

Addie heard the clink-a-clink of Bessie's cowbell near the window. She must have gotten loose, because Pa never let her come this close to the house.

What if Bessie got lost in the storm or buried in a sand drift? Addie pressed her ear to the door, listening for voices, but the fierce wind was all she heard. Addie remembered Ma's words: "Don't go out for anything." Should she disobey and take a look, or just wait? Pa loved that cow. If anything happened to Bessie, Pa would be more than upset.

Addie opened the door and peeked out, but it was dark as night. She plunked William in his crib, wrapped a towel around his head, and cautiously stepped out into the storm.

Swirling grit pelted Addie's face. "Bessie!" she yelled, "Bessie!"

Addie reached out, groping through the sandy air. When her hand touched something rough, she pulled back. Bessie mooed. She touched the cow again, feeling for Bessie's collar. When she found it, she pulled with all her might, but Bessie wouldn't budge. She found Bessie's rump and gave it a slap. Bessie took a step, then another, until Addie managed to push the scrawny cow into the kitchen.

Addie strained to latch the door, but the powerful wind ripped it off its hinges. She screamed. William wailed.

Addie tried to think. Her hands shook as she looked around for a safe place from the wind. Then she remembered the root cellar. Gently stroking Bessie's neck to calm her, Addie managed to coax the cow down the few steps into the dark cellar. Then she went back for William.

"Mama!" he whimpered. "I want Mama!"

"Me, too," said Addie, bolting the door behind her. Addie hugged William to reassure him—and herself, too. She sang songs and played finger games with him while the wind howled on the other side of the door.

After a while, William asked, "Where's Mama?"

Addie's heart beat faster. Surely Ma and Pa should be back by now, but all she heard were thumps and bangs as the wind whipped through the kitchen above her.

Suddenly, everything grew quiet. Addie quickly unlatched the door. It wouldn't open! Sand trickled through the crack at the bottom.

Addie pounded on the door. "Ma! Pa!" she shouted. William wailed. Bessie mooed. But no one came.

Go On

Addie sagged against the dirt wall. They were trapped, alone, in the dark. Ma and Pa were gone. Who would ever look for her? Tears spilled down her cheeks. Then Pa's voice echoed in her head. "When things get tough, we stick it through."

Addie wiped away the tears. What could she do? She could help William. She picked him up, settled him on her lap, and rocked. "Sh, sh," she said. "W-we'll be all right. Ma and Pa will come."

William was almost asleep when Addie heard someone call, "Addie! Where are you?"

"In here!" she hollered, banging on the door. She heard Pa's shovel scrape onto the sand. In a few minutes, Pa pulled the door back so the children could squeeze through. Ma hugged them tight.

Addie blinked at the sunlight. Everything looked topsy-turvy. Sand filled the kitchen. Cups and plates were everywhere, and one of Pa's big old work socks rested in William's dish.

"Your pa got hit with a tree limb," Ma said. "I dragged him into the barn, but the wind was so fierce, I couldn't get back to the house. I kept praying you children were safe."

Addie shuffled to the doorway. The top of Pa's plow poked through the sand. Part of the barn roof was gone. She turned to her father. "I saved Bessie, Pa. Your sweet, wonderful girl is in the root cellar, probably chewing up all our turnips."

Pa grinned, swept Addie up, and swung her around. Addie's mouth dropped open. She giggled with dizziness. Her Pa, always so serious, had never done anything like this.

"You're my sweet, wonderful girl," he said, turning his face, but not before Addie noticed the tears in his eyes.

Go On

1 The author never tells you when this story takes place. Based on details from the story, the best inference is that the events occur

A   in the future
B   about 75 to 150 years ago
C   today
D   about 1000-2000 years ago

2 At the beginning of the story, how does Addie feel about Pa's calling the cow "my sweet, wonderful girl"?

F   She thinks it's cute.
G   She thinks it's a silly name.
H   She feels a little jealous and hurt.
J   It makes her feel happy.

3 Why does Addie decide to go out into the storm?

A   She is worried about Bessie.
B   She wants to look for her mother.
C   The baby is crying.
D   She wants to feel the wind in her hair.

4 All of the following events happened before Addie and William are trapped in the root cellar EXCEPT

F   Pa calls Addie his "sweet, wonderful girl."
G   Bessie coaxes Bessie down the stairs.
H   Pa gets hit with a tree limb.
J   Ma goes out into the storm.

5 Look at the word web below. Which of the following words best fits in the empty circle?

A   Quitter
B   Coward
C   Courageous
D   Tall

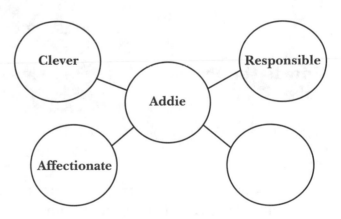

LESSON 8   Plot and Theme

Remember This!

● ● ● ● ● ● ● ● ● ● ● ● ●

Plot

What was the plot of that movie? Did that book have a good plot? Was the plot exciting? How many times have you asked your friends questions like these?

Plot is the plan for what happens in the story. Often the plot starts when the main character has a problem. Then the plot follows the sequence of events that take place as the problem is solved. The story ends with the solution to the problem.

What Is the Problem?	Addie feels sad because she thinks that Pa loves Bessie the cow more than he loves his family.
What Happens to Solve the Problem?	1. Pa and Ma go out into the wind storm. 2. Addie rescues Bessie. 3. The kitchen door is blown off its hinges. 4. Addie brings Bessie and William down to the root cellar. 5. They get trapped in the cellar. 6. Pa and Ma return home and let them out.
How Is the Problem Solved?	Pa feels so proud of Addie that he calls her his "sweet, wonderful girl."

Theme

Theme is much more than what the story is about. It is more than what happens. It is the story's meaning. It is the insight into life you gain after reading the story.

For example, you probably realized that "Pa's Wonderful Girl" tells you something about courage and not giving up. You, like Addie, probably remember Pa's words, "When things get tough, we stick it through." You may have seen that Pa calls Addie his "sweet, wonderful girl" at the end because she was so brave. All of this helps you to see the theme of the story. "Pa's Wonderful Girl" shows that it is important to be brave and show courage during difficult times.

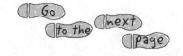

ACTIVITY

Directions Think about a fairy tale or folk tale you have read.
Write a summary of the plot.

_____

_____

_____

_____

ACTIVITY

Directions Use the questions below to help you plan your
own story about bravery.

1. **Theme.** What do you want the story to say about bravery?

_____

_____

2. **Main Character.** Who is the main character in the story?

_____

_____

3. **Problem.** What problem does the main character need to solve?

_____

_____

4. **Action.** What happens to solve the problem?

_____

_____

5. **Solution.** What finally happens? How is the problem solved?

_____

_____

Remember This!

• • • • • • • • • • • • • •

Poetry is written in lines. The end of a line of poetry is not always the end of a sentence. The punctuation marks that tell you that you have come to the end of a sentence are a period (.), a question mark (?), and an exclamation mark (!).

Winter Moon
Langston Hughes

How thin and sharp is the moon tonight!
How thin and sharp and ghostly white
Is the slim curved crook of the moon tonight!

The poem above has three lines, but it has only two sentences. The exclamation mark shows you where each sentence ends. It also indicates surprise, or excitement, or other strong feeling.

Other punctuation marks tell you to take a short pause between lines. These are the comma (,) and the dash (--). They say, "Don't stop! Just pause to take a quick breath." In "Winter Moon," there is no punctuation mark at the end of the second line. This means that you shouldn't pause, but go right on and read the third line.

ACTIVITY

Directions   Read "The Blues." Pay attention to punctuation marks that indicate the end of a sentence. Also notice when you should take a short pause at the end of a line and when you should go right on to the next line. Then answer the questions.

The Blues
Langston Hughes

When the shoe strings break
On both your shoes
And you're in a hurry—
That's the blues.

When you go to buy a candy bar
And you've lost the dime you had—
Slipped through a hole in your pocket somewhere—
That's the blues, too, and bad!

1. This poem has how many sentences?_____

2. This poem has how many lines?_____

3. What does the dash at the end of the third line tell you to do?

_____

4. What does the period at the end of the fourth line tell you to do?

_____

5. What does the exclamation mark at the end of the last line tell you to do?

_____

ACTIVITY

Directions   "The Blues" is a fun poem to read aloud. Practice reading it on your own. Let the punctuation marks guide you. Remember that they will tell you when to pause, when to stop, and when to say a line with extra expression. Then read the poem aloud to your classmates.

LESSON 10   Apply to the Test

You've learned a lot about plot and theme and using punctuation to read poetry. Here are samples of test questions dealing with these skills.

Directions
Read "The Owl and the Pussycat." Then do Numbers 1-5.

The Owl and the Pussycat
Edward Lear

The Owl and the Pussycat went to sea
   In a beautiful pea-green boat,
They took some honey, and plenty of money,
   Wrapped up in a five-pound note.
The Owl looked up to the stars above,
   And sang to a small guitar,
"O lovely Pussy! O Pussy, my love
   What a beautiful Pussy you are,
      You are,
      You are!
What a beautiful Pussy you are!"

Pussy said to the Owl, "You elegant fowl!"
   How charmingly sweet you sing!
O let us to marry! too long we have tarried:
   But what shall we do for a ring?"
They sailed away, for a year and a day,
   To the land where the Bong-tree grows,
And there in the wood a Piggy-wig stood
   With a ring at the end of his nose,
      His nose,
      His nose,
   With a ring at the end of his nose.

Go On

"Dear Pig, are you willing to sell for one shilling
  Your ring?" Said the Piggy, "I will."
So they took it away, and were married next day
  By the Turkey who lives on the hill.
They dined on mince, and slices of quince,
  Which they ate with a runcible spoon;
And hand-in-hand, on the edge of the sand,
  They danced by the light of the moon,
      The moon,
      The moon,
  They danced by the light of the moon.

Sample Plot Questions

1 **The Owl and the Pussycat want to get married, but they have a problem. What is it?**

A They don't have a ring.
B They don't have enough money.
C They can't find a preacher.
D None of the above.

2 **What happens that helps them solve their problem?**

F The Owl proposes to the Pussycat.
G They sail away in a beautiful pea green boat.
H They meet a Piggy-wig.
J They dine on mince.

Sample Theme Question

3 **Which of the following would be another good title for this poem?**

A The Turkey Who Lives on the Hill
B A Ring for His Nose
C An Animal Love Story
D The Light of the Moon

Sample Reading Poetry Questions

4 **How does the poet want you to read the line, "What a beautiful Pussy you are!"?**

F as a question
G with emphasis
H as a statement
J by running it into the next line

5 **How many sentences are there in the first stanza?**

A one
B two
C three
D four

Directions Read the poem. Then do Numbers 1-5 on the next page.

There's Always Weather
Langston Hughes

There's always weather, weather,
Whether we like it or not.
Some days are nice and sunny,
Sunny and bright and hot.

There's always weather, weather,
Whether we like it or don't.
Sometimes so cold and cloudy!
Will it soon snow, or won't?

If days were always just the same,
Out-of-doors would be so tame—
Never a wild and windy day,
Never a stormy sky of gray.

I'm glad there's weather, whether,
Dark days, then days full of sun.
Summer and fall and winter—
Weather is so much fun!

1 The poet uses two homophones in this poem. *Homophones* are words that sound the same but have different spellings and different meanings. The first homophone is *weather*, which means "the general state of the outside air." What is the meaning of *whether*?

A if
B stormy conditions
C except
D sunny

2 Another good title for this poem is

F Clouds Above Me
G Weather Is Fun
H Wild and Windy Days
J Changing the Weather

3 The poet seems to want

A all days to be the same.
B the weather to change from day to day.
C every day to be bright and sunny.
D every day to be wild and windy.

4 *Mood* is the feeling created by a work of literature. Which word best describes the mood of this poem?

F joyful
G sad
H angry
J peaceful

5 The last line ends with an exclamation mark. This mark tells you to

A pause briefly
B show strong feeling
C ask a question
D none of the above

ACTIVITIES

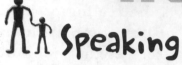

Speaking

"The Hungry Goddess" is a great story to read aloud. Practice performing an oral reading of it. Pay special attention to how you would say, "Tengo hambre." Stretch out the syllables in these words. Remember that she is soooooo hungry.

Give the hungry goddess personality. Make her whine and wail. Make her moan and cry. Remember that her cry is so annoying that the gods can't sleep. Once you feel comfortable, perform your oral reading for your classmates. You might invite them to join in when you call out, "Tengo hambre."

_____

_____

_____

_____

Writing

Try your hand at writing a poem. First think of a topic you would like to write about. Then create a word web to describe this topic. Use these words to create a vivid word picture of your topic. You might decide to have the words at the end of lines rhyme. After you have finished drafting your poem, check it for correct spelling, punctuation, and grammar.

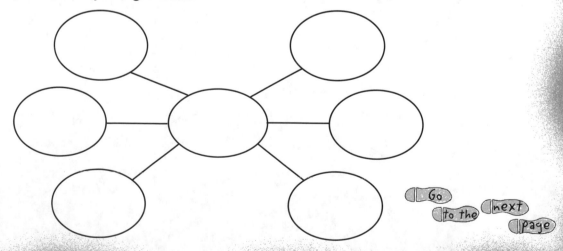

Go to the next page

Measuring Up™ to the New York State Learning Standards

ACTIVITIES

 Reading

Start keeping a personal reading journal. Select a notebook to write in. Decorate the cover to make it your own. For each book you read, fill out the following information.

Title_____

Author_____

Date Read _____

Main Characters _____

What It Was About _____

Would I Recommend It to Someone Else?_____

Listening

Listen to a reading of a story on the radio or on tape. As you listen, jot down notes to keep track of the characters' names. Indicate what they are like. Tell what they do. Later tell your classmates whether you found the reading effective.

_____

_____

_____

_____

_____

_____

_____

_____

_____

WRITING TO DEMONSTRATE UNDERSTANDING

UNIT 2

What's Expected on the New York State English Language Arts Test?

You're now ready for the writing part of the New York State English Language Arts Test. What will you be expected to do?

On Day 1, you showed your reading comprehension by answering multiple choice questions. On Days 2 and 3, you will show your understanding through writing.

On Day 2, you will listen to a passage and write two short responses and one longer response. Then you will write a composition. On Day 3, you will read two articles and write responses to them.

So in this unit, you'll start with the big picture and master the stages of the writing process. Then you will develop the tools you need to listen and read effectively and write your responses.

By the end of these chapters, you will be able to

* **Listen to a story**
* **Read and connect information in two stories**
* **Show your understanding by writing detailed responses to questions**
* **Use standard grammar, spelling, and punctuation**

Keys to Success

How will your responses be judged? What is a good response? Here are the points people will look for as they read your response. Don't worry too much about these points now. You will be learning a lot about them in this unit. Keep them in the back of your mind as you work through these chapters.

Meaning

A good response shows that you have understood the passage. Here, you are ahead of the game. In Chapters 1 and 2, you worked on building your comprehension skills. A good response also shows that you have understood the writing prompt, or question. This makes sense, doesn't it? Make sure you have answered the question that was asked.

Development

A good response is well developed. It uses information to back up ideas. This is your chance to show how much you know. If you provide only a little information, people will think you don't know very much about the subject. If you provide information that doesn't support the main idea, it won't count.

Organization

A good response is well organized. In this unit, you will learn how to begin with a topic sentence and end with a conclusion. You will learn how to organize your ideas using time order, cause and effect, and comparison and contrast.

Language Use

Language use refers to how well you use the English language. A good response uses words and sentences well. Good writers think about the words they use. They choose the ones that best carry their meaning. They hold their readers' interest by varying their sentences.

Conventions

Conventions are the rules of a language. A good response shows that you know the rules of grammar, spelling, capitalization and punctuation. Always read over your writing to check for these four things. It's a shame to have points taken off because you've made a careless spelling error. Take the time to make sure your response shines.

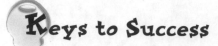

Keys to Success

ACTIVITY

Directions Discuss each of these points with your classmates.
Make a list of reasons why you think each point is important.

1. Meaning _____

    _____

    _____

    _____

2. Development _____

    _____

    _____

    _____

3. Organization _____

    _____

    _____

    _____

4. Language Use _____

    _____

    _____

    _____

5. Conventions _____

    _____

    _____

    _____

     Measuring Up™ to the New York State Learning Standards

Chapter 3   THE WRITING PROCESS

What's It All About?

In this chapter, you will learn

✱ what is the writing process

✱ how to prewrite

✱ how to draft

✱ how to revise your writing

✱ how to proofread your writing

✱ how to publish and share your writing

What Is the Writing Process?

Good writing doesn't just spring into your head full blown. It needs to be developed through a series of stages or steps.

A process is a series of steps that lead to a result. The series of steps that lead to a finished piece of writing is called the *writing process*.

Stages of the Writing Process

Prewriting

The first stage is called *prewriting*. Think of this as the idea stage. This is when you come up with a topic and brainstorm ideas to flesh out that topic. It's when you make decisions such as what your purpose is for writing and who your audience is. It is when you gather information by reading, listening, and viewing.

Drafting

The second stage is called *drafting*. Think of this as the "first try" stage. Here you give shape to your writing by organizing your words and sentences. You elaborate and provide support for your ideas. Of course, you may want to take a "second try" and a "third try" or as many "tries" as you like.

Revising

The third stage is called revising. Think of this as the improving or polishing stage. Here you take the time to make your writing even better. You look at it with a reader's eye and determine what changes need to be made. You look at your vocabulary and your sentence structure to make your writing stronger.

Go to the next page

Proofreading

The fourth stage is called proofreading. Think of this as the fixing stage. Here you check your grammar, punctuation, and spelling. You make sure you have followed the conventions of writing.

Publishing

The last stage is called publishing. Think of this as the pay off. Why have you written something in the first place? You've written it so that someone can read it or hear it or see it. This is your opportunity to share your thoughts with others.

ACTIVITY

Directions Try to help your classmates. Think about how you write. Write down three things you do that help you to write successfully. Share them with your classmates. Then work together as a group to create a list called *Tips for Successful Writers*.

_____

_____

_____

_____

_____

_____

_____

_____

_____

LESSON 1   Prewriting

Choose Your Topic

The *topic* is what you are writing about. The topic may be a person, place, thing, or idea. Before you write about something, you have to decide what that something is. Sometimes the topic is given to you in an assignment. Sometimes you can select your own topic—one that especially interests you. For example, you might choose the topic *Dogs*.

Next, you narrow or focus your topic. *Dogs* is a very big topic. Certainly, you could write a book about just dogs. Focus your topic. Decide what part of this big topic you want to cover. For example, you might narrow the topic *Dogs* to *How Dogs Communicate*.

Once you have your topic, decide what point you want to make. This is something interesting that you want to say. It is your *main idea*. For example, you might make your point: *A dog's actions speak louder than words*.

Topic:	Dogs
Focused Topic:	How Dogs Communicate
Point or Main Idea:	A dog's actions speak louder than words.

LESSON 1   Prewriting

ACTIVITY

Directions Imagine you are writing a composition for social studies. Follow the steps to answer each of the questions below.

STEP 1
Choose Your Topic.

1. What topic would you like to write about?

_____

STEP 2
Focus your topic.

2. How would you focus this topic? Write your focused topic on the line below.

_____

STEP 3
Decide what point you want to make about your topic.

3. What is one point you might make about your topic?

_____

4. What is a different point you might make about this topic?

_____

ACTIVITY

Directions Imagine you are writing a paper for science. Answer the questions below.

1. What topic would you like to write about?_____

_____

2. How would you focus this topic? Write your focused topic on the line below.

_____

3. What is one point you might make about your topic?

_____

4. What is a different point you might make about this topic?

_____

       Measuring Up™ to the New York State Learning Standards

LESSON 2   Prewriting

Decide on Your Audience and Purpose

• • • • • • • • • • • • • •

Before you start writing, decide on your audience and your purpose for writing. The person or group of people who are going to read or listen to what you write is called your audience. Here are some question to ask yourself about your audience.

> Who is going to read this or listen to this?
>
> How much do they already know about the topic?
>
> How much do they need to know to understand the topic?

Your purpose for writing is your reason. Here are some purposes you might have for writing.

Inform	You want to give your audience information about something.
Instruct	You want to tell your audience how to do something.
Entertain	You want to make your audience laugh or feel sad or feel suspense and excitement.
Persuade	You want to make your audience believe something or do something.

Go to the next page

LESSON 2   Prewriting

ACTIVITY

Directions You have been asked to write a paragraph to teach other fourth graders to play checkers. It will be used by children at the community center. Read the steps and answer the questions.

STEP 1

Identify your purpose for writing.

1. Why are you writing this piece?_____
_____

2. What do you want your readers to get from it?_____
_____

STEP 2

Identify your readers, or audience.

3. Who will be reading your paragraph?_____
_____

4. What will they want to find out from reading it?_____
_____

STEP 3

Decide how to write to achieve your purpose.

5. Which of the following sentences would make the best first sentence? Explain how this sentence helps you achieve your purpose.

Checkers is the best game in the world.

Checkers is a board game for two players.

Checkers has been a popular game for thousands of years.

_____
_____
_____
_____

Go to the next page

     Measuring Up™ to the New York State Learning Standards

ACTIVITY

Directions Read the paragraph below. Then answer the questions at the end of it.

William Carlos Williams had two successful jobs. He wrote poetry and he worked as a doctor. He cared for children for more than forty years. As he made house calls, he picked up ideas for his poems. He described the land and the change of seasons. He wrote about people's troubles and dreams. Being a doctor made Williams a better poet.

1. Who or what is the topic of this paragraph? _____

_____

2. Does this paragraph persuade, inform, entertain, or instruct? _____

_____

3. Who would make the best audience for this paragraph?
   Explain your choice.

   a. a Spanish club

   b. a poetry club

   c. a group of doctors

   d. a softball team

_____

_____

4. Which sentence best fits in this paragraph?
   Explain how this sentence helps you achieve your purpose.

   a. Many poems have short lines that rhyme.

   b. William Carlos Williams is the greatest American poet.

   c. As a doctor and a poet, Williams was interested in how people felt.

   d. Traveling over country roads can be tough.

_____

_____

LESSON 3 Prewriting

Brainstorm Ideas

Probably, you already know a lot about your topic. Brainstorming is a good way of coming up with ideas about a topic based on what you already know. Think of brainstorming as an explosion of ideas in your mind.

The goal of brainstorming is to get down on paper as many ideas as you can. Put down anything you think of. Don't worry if your ideas are good or not. Then make connections between these ideas. Finally select from them the ones you think you would like to include in your composition

A good tool for brainstorming is a web. Look below to see how brainstorming is done.

STEP 1

Write the topic in a circle

STEP 2

Try to come up with as many ideas as you can about your topic. Write them in circles around your topic.

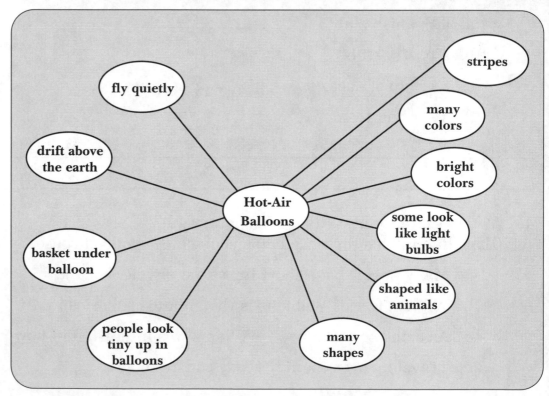

Go to the next page

STEP 3

Make connections between your ideas. Draw lines between ideas that go together.

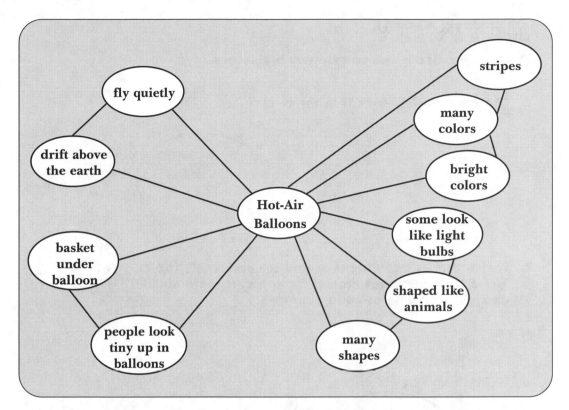

STEP 4

Select ideas you want to be sure to include in your composition. Notice the star next to ideas to include.

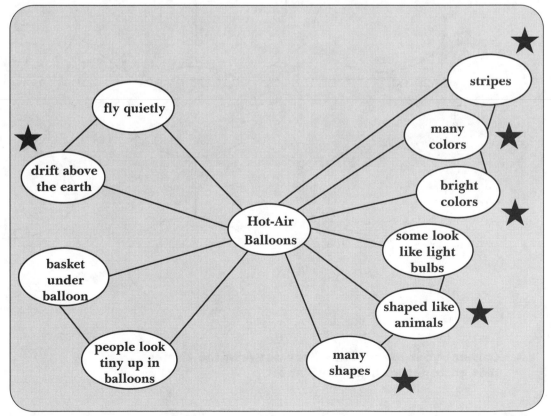

Go to the next page

ACTIVITY

Directions Use a web to help you brainstorm.

1. Choose a topic. Write it in the circle.

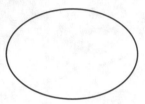

2. Brainstorm as many ideas as you can about this topic. Write them in circles around the topic. If there aren't enough circles below, add your own.

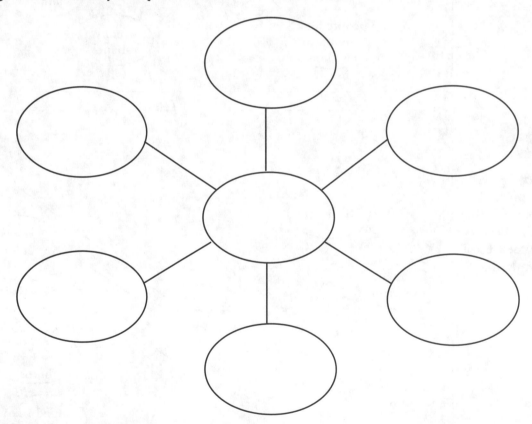

3. Connect your ideas. Draw lines between the circles that go together in the web above.

4. Look over your web. Star any ideas you would like to use in a composition.

LESSON 4 Prewriting

Gather Information

Some ideas come to mind very easily. Usually, that's because they are based on things you already know. Others take more time and work. You need to gather information from other sources before the ideas start flowing. These sources can be things you see, things you read, and things you listen to.

Before you start to write, take an inventory of what you know about your topic and what you want to know. Also indicate how you can find out the information you need.

For example, imagine your topic is *chameleons*. Here is an example of how to gather information.

STEP 1

Jot down what you already know about the topic.

> a type of lizard
> changes color to match its surroundings
> hard to spot
> has a long tongue
> eats insects

STEP 2

Jot down questions you have about the topic. These questions should tell what you want to find out.

> Where does it live?
>
> How does it change color?
>
> What type of insects does it eat?
>
> What are some other lizards?

STEP 3

Write down sources you can use to find this information.

> encyclopedia
> book on lizards
> documentary video on lizards
> field guide

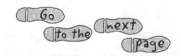
Go to the next page

LESSON 4 Prewriting

ACTiViTY

Directions Now try it yourself. First decide on your topic. Then fill out the chart below.

Topic _____

What Do You Know?	What Do You Want to Know?	How Can You Find Out?

Take Notes

• • • • • • • • • • • • •

Can you remember details about what you read, see, or hear? It's impossible to remember everything. A good way to remember is to take notes. Good notes cover only the most important points.

ACTIVITY

Directions: Read the paragraph below. Then follow the steps for taking notes to answer the questions.

Wildflowers are known for their beauty, but they are also quite useful. Wildflowers delight the eye with their vivid colors. Colorful plants such as wild indigo and bloodroot can be used to dye clothing. And what about their lovely scent? Wildflowers such as violets and honeysuckle are used to make perfumes. Wildflowers have other useful purposes, too. Some wildflowers such as wild roses and mint are used to make teas. The seeds of the pretty yellow flower black mustard give us the mustard we use to add flavor to foods, while sunflowers give us those crunchy seeds that we sprinkle on salads for flavor. Striped wintergreen and wild sarsaparilla are used to flavor candy and soda. Wildflowers are used in medicines, too. Foxglove is used in heart medicine and Butter-and-Eggs is used to treat eye infections. Next time you take a walk in the woods, think about all the uses for wildflowers.

STEP 1

Identify the main idea of the paragraph. The sentence that tells you the main idea is called the topic sentence.

1. Who or what is the topic of this paragraph?_____

_____

2. What is the main idea you learned about this topic? Write down the topic sentence._____

_____

_____

Go to the next page

STEP 2

Find important details that back up the main idea.

3. Write five important details that support the main idea.

_____

_____

_____

_____

_____

STEP 3

Put your notes in outline form. Keep the details short. Tell only what's needed to remember the point. In the outline below, fill in the missing details.

I. **Uses of Wildflowers**

    A. **Dye for clothing**
       1. wild indigo
       2. bloodroot

    B. **Perfume**
       1. violets
       2. _____

    C. **Teas**
       1. _____
       2. mint

    D. **Flavor**
       1. _____
       2 _____
       3 _____
       4 _____

    E. _____
       1. foxglove
       2. _____

4. How would this outline help you give a talk about uses of wildflowers?

_____

_____

Measuring Up™ to the New York State Learning Standards

LESSON 6   Drafting

Organize Through Time Order

Think about the activities you did during the prewriting stage. You chose your topic, focused it, and came up with your main point, or idea. You thought about your audience and your purpose. You brainstormed ideas and collected information from other sources.

Now you are ready to write your first draft. How do you organize your thoughts on paper? How do you put your sentences in an order that makes sense?

One way to organize your writing is time order. Time order means putting your sentences in the order in which the events occur. You might want to use time order when you are writing a story, a biography, an autobiography, a history, or directions.

ACTIVITY

Directions Follow the steps to organize a paragraph by time order.

STEP 1

Start with a topic sentence. This is the sentence that tells you the main idea.

The sailboats we call Hudson River sloops have a long history.

1. What is the topic of this paragraph going to be?

_____

2. Write the main idea in your own words.

_____

_____

_____

_____

Go to the next page

STEP 2

Organize the sentences that support the main idea in time order.

3. The sentences below are out of order. Put 1 by the event that happens first, 2 by the event that happens second, and so on.

_____ By the 1850s, steamboats took over from the sloops.

_____ In the early 1800s villages along the Hudson used sloops to carry goods to market.

_____ When New York was still New Amsterdam, Dutch captains built Hudson River sloops to sail up the river.

_____ The golden days of the Hudson River sloop are not forgotten. In 1969, the Clearwater was built for the Hudson River Sloop Revival.

_____ These sloops were hearty sailing vessels. In 1785, owners of a Hudson Valley sloop sailed from New York to China.

STEP 3

End your paragraph with a strong conclusion.

4. Write a conclusion for this paragraph.

_____

_____

_____

_____

_____

_____

_____

_____

_____

_____

_____

LESSON 7   Drafting

Organize Through Cause and Effect

A nother way to organize your writing is through cause and effect. A *cause* is what makes something happen. An *effect* is what happens. In other words, an effect is the result of the cause.

For example, the sentence below tells an effect or result:

My mother's beautiful glass vase broke.

Here is the cause:

The cat jumped on the table and knocked it over.

Why did the glass vase break? It broke because the cat knocked it over.

Organize your paragraph through cause and effect when you want to answer the question "Why?" or "What would happen if?"

ACTIVITY

Directions Follow the steps below to organize a paragraph by cause and effect.

STEP 1

Begin with a sentence that tells the result.

There are several reasons why war broke out between Britain and the thirteen colonies.

1. What is the topic of this paragraph?

_____

2. Write a sentence restating the main idea.

_____

_____

Go to the next page

STEP 2

Write sentences that explain the causes. In other words, give the reasons that led to the result.

3. Read the sentences below. Write "Yes" by any sentence that gives a cause. This is a sentence you would use in this paragraph. Write "No" by any sentence that does not.

_____ Britain put taxes on goods the colonists needed.

_____ The colonists felt they had little say in how they were being governed.

_____ George Washington was a brave general.

_____ New York was one of the thirteen original colonies.

_____ Colonists had to pay for boarding and feeding British troops on our shores.

STEP 3

End with a conclusion that restates, or says in different words, your main idea.

4. Write a conclusion for this paragraph.

_____

_____

_____

_____

_____

_____

_____

_____

_____

_____

_____

Go to the next page

Another way to write a cause and effect paragraph is to start with the cause. Then provide sentences that give several effects resulting from this cause.

ACTIVITY

Directions Follow the steps below to write a cause and effect paragraph.

STEP 1

Write a topic sentence that gives a cause.

> *Moving lunch hour from 11:30 to 12:30 has had several bad effects.*

1. What is the topic of this paragraph? This topic is the cause.

_____

2. Restate the main idea in your own words.

_____

STEP 2

Write three or four sentences that tell the effects of this cause.

3. Write "Yes" by any sentence above that states an effect. These are the sentences you would use in your paragraph. Write "No" by any sentence that does not.

_____ Most students in my class get hungry around 11:00 o'clock.

_____ 12:30 is too late to eat lunch.

_____ Many students have their mind on food, not on the subject they are learning.

_____ Younger children get sleepy when they have to wait so long for lunch.

_____ The cafeteria could use more seats.

STEP 3

End your paragraph with a sentence that restates the main idea.

4. Write a conclusion restating the main idea.

_____

_____

_____

LESSON 8 Drafting

Organize Through Comparison and Contrast

When you *compare* two things, you should show how they are the same. When you *contrast* two things, you should show how they are different. Another way to organize your paragraph is through comparison and contrast. You organize a paragraph this way when you want to show likenesses and differences.

ACTIVITY

Directions **Follow the steps below to organize a paragraph through comparison and contrast.**

STEP 1

Start with a topic sentence. The topic sentence will introduce two things that you will compare and contrast.

Two of my favorite novels are based on the folktale Cinderella.

1. What is the topic of this paragraph? In other words, what two things will be compared and contrasted?

   _____

2. Restate the main idea in your own words.

   _____

STEP 2

Write sentences that show how these two things are the same and how they are different.

3. Write "compare" by any sentence above that shows how Becan and Bubba are alike. Write "contrast" by any sentence that shows how they are different.

   _____ *The Irish Cinderlad* was written by Shirley Climo, while *Bubba the Cowboy Prince* was written by Helen Kelleman.

   _____ In both *The Irish Cinderlad* and *Bubba the Cowboy Prince*, the Cinderella-like character is a boy.

   _____ In both tales, the fairy godmother is actually a magical cow.

   _____ One tale is set in Ireland, while the other takes place in Texas.

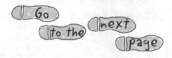
Go to the next page

Copying is illegal.   Measuring Up™ to the New York State Learning Standards

STEP 2
(continued)

_____ *The Irish Cinderlad* takes place on a farm, while *Bubba the Cowboy Prince* takes place on a ranch.

_____ Both Becan, the Irish Cinderlad, and Bubba lose a piece of footware—a boot.

_____ Both characters marry and live happily ever after.

_____ But Becan marries a princess, while Bubba marries the owner of a large ranch in Texas.

STEP 3

End your paragraph with a strong conclusion.

4. Write a conclusion for this paragraph.

_____

_____

ACTIVITY

Directions **Now try it on your own.**

1. Choose one of the following topics or make up your own.
    Write your topic on the line below.

    two characters from two novels you have read
    two baseball heroes
    taking a vacation at the beach or in the mountain
    ice cream and sherbet

_____

2. Write a topic sentence.

_____

3. Write four sentences showing how these two things are alike
    and how they are different.

_____

_____

_____

4. Write a conclusion for your paragraph.

_____

LESSON 9 Drafting

Elaborate

Y ou've written your first draft. Take time to read it over. Have you provided enough information to support your main idea? Do you need to elaborate, or add more detail?

In order to add more detail, you may need to

* �֎ brainstorm some more
* ✖ gather information by talking to people
* ✖ gather information from reading, writing, or viewing

ACTIVITY

Directions Read the paragraph below. It is too skimpy or thin. It needs more detail. Decide which details you would include in this paragraph. Write "Yes" by any detail you would include. Write "No" by any detail you would not include because it does not support the main idea.

Alexander Hamilton played an important role in the history of the United States. He helped to get the U.S. Constitution accepted by all states. He served as Secretary of the Treasury when George Washington was president. Alexander Hamilton was a great American.

1. ____ Hamilton wrote a series of papers that made people want to support the Constitution.

2. ____ Hamilton fought a duel with Aaron Burr.

3. ____ The first capital of the United States was New York City.

4. ____ Hamilton helped Thomas Jefferson get elected president in 1801.

5. ____ Hamilton represented New York at the convention where the Constitution was written.

6. ____ Hamilton started the First Bank of the United States.

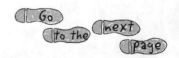
Go to the next page

7. ____ Hamilton was married to Elizabeth Schuyler.

8. ____ The Schuyler family was wealthy.

9. ____ Hamilton's ideas about a strong central government still influence people today.

10. ____ Hamilton also worked as George Washington's secretary during the Revolutionary War.

ACTIVITY

Directions Read the paragraph below. It is too skimpy or thin. Write four sentences with details you would add to this paragraph.

I always have a good time when I go to an amusement park. The roller coasters are my favorite ride. I like the excitement of slowly going up a steep hill and then zooming down. I also like the giant slides. Visiting an amusement park is a great way to spend a summer day.

1. _____

_____

_____

2. _____

_____

_____

3. _____

_____

_____

4. _____

_____

_____

LESSON 10 Revision

Use Varied Words

● ● ● ● ● ● ● ● ● ● ● ●

How many words can you think of that mean *storm*? You might list the words *blizzard, tornado, thunderstorm,* or *northeaster*. Each of these words is a different kind of storm.

How many words can you think of that mean *edge.* Could you come up with *rim, brink, boundary,* and *border*?

Often people use words that are not exact. Sometimes they use the same word over and over again. Words that are not exact may confuse readers. Using the same words again and again is boring. Good writers change, or vary, the words they use to say exactly what they mean and to keep their readers interested.

ACTIVITY

Directions Read the paragraph below. Then follow the steps to answer the questions.

STEP 1

Identify words that are overused.

People **talk** in many different ways. Usually, we think of **talking** as using our voices. But sign language lets people **talk** by using their hands. This is particularly helpful when **talking** with someone who doesn't hear well. People also **talk** through body language. Everyone knows what it means when you shake your head up and down or from left to right. Many other body actions **talk** as loudly as words. Usually we think someone is **talking** the truth when this person looks us in the eye. We think someone is sad when she hangs her head low. We think someone is embarrassed if he blushes bright red. A wave can **talk**, too. It can say hello or goodbye. We also **talk** through touch. A hug **talks** that we like someone. A kiss **talks** words of affection. How many ways have you talked today?

1. In the paragraph above, which words are written in boldface?

   _____

2. How many times is each of these words repeated?_____

   _____

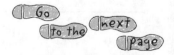

STEP 2

Find words that are more varied and interesting.

3. Synonyms are words that have the same or almost the same meaning. Use your dictionary to add two synonyms to each list.

talk	talking
speak	speaking
tell	telling
communicate	communicating
_____	_____
_____	_____

STEP 3

Decide which word would be more interesting to a reader.

4. Rewrite the paragraph using synonyms to replace the overused words.

_____

_____

_____

_____

_____

_____

_____

_____

_____

_____

_____

_____

_____

_____

LESSON 11 Revision

Use Varied Sentences

When you begin every sentence the same way, your writing may seem boring. This also occurs when all of your sentences are about the same length. One way to spice up your writing is to vary your sentence patterns.

For example, read the paragraph below. Notice that every sentence begins the same way. Each sentence begins with a subject. Also notice how all the sentences are about the same length.

Fingerprints are made up of ridges. These ridges look like arches, loops, and whorls. Fingerprints do not change with time. You have fingerprints at age 10. You have the same fingerprints at age 20. Fingerprints help detectives solve crimes. No two people have the same fingerprints.

Now notice how the paragraph gets more interesting when you vary the sentence pattern.

Fingerprints are made up of ridges that look like arches, loops, and whorls. Fingerprints do not change with time. The fingerprints you have at age 10 are the same as the ones you will have at age 20. Since no two people have the same fingerprints, they can help detectives solve crimes.

ACTIVITY

Directions Follow these steps to vary your sentence pattern.

Read over your writing. Ask yourself these questions.

✱ Do all my sentences begin the same way?

✱ Are all my sentences the same length?

✱ Does my writing sound monotonous, or boring, when I read it out loud?

 Measuring Up™ to the New York State Learning Standards

LESSON 11   Revision

STEP 1
(continued)

1. Answer the questions on page 96 about both paragraphs on fingerprints.

Paragraph 1 _____

_____

_____

Paragraph 2 _____

_____

_____

STEP 2

Combine sentences to vary length.

2. Combine each pair of sentences below by using the word *and*, *but*, or *or*. Put a comma in place of the first period. Lowercase the first letter of the word after *and*, *but*, or *or*.

   Example

   You can play ball at Roberto Clemente State Park. You can ride a carousel at Riverbank State Bank.

   <u>becomes</u>

   You can play ball at Roberto Clemente State Park, and you can ride a carousel at Riverbank State Park.

a. Watching baseball is fun. Playing baseball is better. _____

_____

b. Marie lives at the lake. Lila lives in town. _____

_____

c. All dogs are fun to play with. Puppies are the best. _____

_____

d. I can go to the movies. I can save my money. _____

_____

e. I hiked in the mountains. I swam in the lake. _____

_____

Go to the next page

STEP 3

Combine sentences to vary the way they begin.

3. Combine each pair of sentences below. Use the word *since*, *because*, or *although* at the beginning of the new sentence. Put a comma in place of the first period. Lowercase the first letter of the first word after the comma.

> *Example*
>
> I ate a big lunch. I was hungry at dinner time.
>
> <u>becomes</u>
>
> Although I ate a big lunch, I was hungry at dinner time.

a. My cat likes to sleep on my clothes. They are covered with white hairs.

_____

_____

b. My parakeet likes to sing at night. It keeps me awake. _____

_____

c. We put the cat on a diet. She still stayed fat. _____

_____

d. Our canary likes to eat cookies and cake. We call her Biscuits.

_____

_____

e. Uncle Pete is scared of our pet snake. He doesn't visit us much any more.

_____

_____

_____

_____

     Measuring Up™ to the New York State Learning Standards

LESSON 12   Revision

Use Other Revision Strategies

How many times have you said, "If only I could do that again. Now I know how to make it better." Revision offers you a special opportunity. You get the chance to go over your writing to make it even better.

ACTIVITY

Directions Follow the steps to revise the paragraph below.

STEP 1

Read over your work with a critic's eye. Step back from it. See it as someone else would see it. Be your own critic.

> My favorite character is Pippi Longstocking, but my best friend likes Ramona better. Pippi lives alone in a villa in Sweden. Ramona lives with her family. Pippi has great adventures. Ramona has good adventures, too. I like other books, too, like *The Dragon Princess* and *Mufaro's Beautiful Daughters*. I guess I just like to read.

1. A good technique for reading with a critic's eye is to read your writing aloud. By hearing how your writing sounds, you begin to think about it differently. Read the paragraph above aloud. How does it sound to you? What are its strengths? What are its weaknesses? Write your comments below.

   _____

   _____

STEP 2

Work with a group of students. You've heard the phrase, "Two heads are better than one." Review your work with others. Ask for their comments and advice.

2. Form a group of four or five students. Talk about the paragraph about Pippi Longstocking and Ramona. Use the following questions to guide your discussion.

   a. Does the beginning of the paragraph grab you? Are the details interesting? What is the most interesting thing about the paragraph? How would you make it more interesting?

   _____

   _____

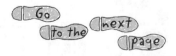
Go to the next page

LESSON 12   Revision

STEP 2
(continued)

b. Can you follow the information easily? Is the paragraph well organized? How would you improve the way it is organized?

_____

_____

c. Do the details support the main idea? Does any information need to be added? Do the details need to be more specific? What else would you like to know?

_____

_____

d. Does any information need to be taken out? Does the writer get off track and start talking about something else?

_____

_____

e. Is any information confusing? How could it be made clearer?

_____

_____

STEP 3

Meet with your teacher. Discuss the strengths of your writing. Also talk about how to make it better.

3. Have a class discussion with your teacher. Write notes below about the strengths and weaknesses of the paragraph and how to make it better.

_____

_____

STEP 4

Keep a portfolio of your writing. Review your work from time to time.

Think about the topics that continue to interest you. Think about what you have written particularly well and what you are pariculary proud of. Think about what you can improve.

4. Choose a notebook or a file folder for your portfolio. Design a cover. Put a title on it; for example, "The Writing of Amanda Brown." Let your cover celebrate you.

LESSON 13 Proofreading

Use Correct Verb Tense

Proofreading is the stage where you check your grammar, spelling, and punctuation. Grammar is the rules that govern how our language works. One common grammar problem is verb tense.

A verb is a word that shows action or a state of being. The verb in the sentence below is italicized.

I *run* fast.

The tense of a verb shows time.

Present: Now I *run* very fast.

Past: Yesterday I *ran* slowly.

Future   Tomorrow I *will run* even faster.

A common problem in writing is mixing up verb tenses. If the events take place in the present, keep your verbs in the present tense. If the events occurred in the past, keep your verbs in the past tense. If the events haven't happened yet but will happen, keep your verbs in the future tense.

ACTIVITY

Directions Underline the verb in each sentence below. Tell whether it is in the past, present, or future tense.

1. Jose ate three peaches.   Tense: _____
2. Michael will go to summer camp.   Tense: _____
3. The author wrote about her childhood.   Tense: _____
4. The child sings sweetly.   Tense: _____
5. He tells silly jokes.   Tense: _____
6. Malcolm has the tickets for the game.   Tense: _____
7. Louise gave her tickets away.   Tense: _____
8. Next week we will go to the tennis match.   Tense: _____
9. Yesterday Patricia forgot her lunch.   Tense: _____
10. I will start the report tonight.   Tense: _____

Go to the next page

LESSON 13 Revision

ACTiViTY

Directions Read the paragraph below. Pay special attention to the underlined verbs. Then answer the questions.

Ancient Egyptians <u>buried</u> their dead pharaohs, or kings, with a lot of ceremony.
1

First priests <u>prepare</u> the dead pharaoh's body. This preparation <u>protected</u> the
2   3

body for the journey to the afterworld. Then they <u>will place</u> the mummified
4

body, or mummy, in a sled. Two women <u>dressed</u> as goddesses <u>will travel</u>
5   6

with the body. Mourners, wearing blue, <u>walked</u> alongside. The mourners <u>wail</u>
7   8

and <u>screeched</u>. They <u>created</u> quite a commotion. Dancers and musicians
9   10

<u>accompanied</u> the mummy, too. Servants <u>carry</u> treasures for the dead pharaoh.
11   12

In the tomb, they <u>put</u> the mummy in a wooden coffin. This coffin <u>looked</u> like
13   14

the pharaoh. Then they <u>placed</u> the coffin in a sarcophagus. They <u>will cover</u> the
15   16

top of the sarcophagus with a stone lid. Finally they <u>sealed</u> the tomb and
17

<u>remove</u> all traces of the burial chamber. But grave robbers still <u>discovered</u> many
18   19

of the tombs and <u>steal</u> the treasures.
20

Several of these verbs are in the wrong tense. Which verbs need to be changed? If the tense of the verb needs to be changed, write the correct form on the line. Which verbs are correct? Write *Correct* next to these.

1. buried _____
2. prepare _____
3. protected _____
4. will place _____
5. dressed _____
6. will travel _____
7. walked _____
8. wail _____
9. screeched _____
10. created _____

11. accompanied _____
12. carry _____
13. put _____
14. looked _____
15. placed _____
16. will cover _____
17. sealed _____
18. remove _____
19. discovered _____
20. steal _____

LESSON 14 Proofreading

Check Your Grammar

W hen you proofread your writing, check your grammar. Here are two more common grammar problems.

Sentence Fragments

What is a complete sentence? A sentence is a group of words with a subject and a predicate, or verb. A sentence always expresses a complete thought. Sometimes people plan to write a sentence, but they leave out one of the parts. A sentence that is incomplete is called a *fragment*.

> **Rule:** Make sure your sentence contains a subject and a verb and expresses a complete thought.

Incorrect

The driver of the third car.

Did what? This sentence lacks a verb.

Correct

The driver of the third car fled.

Incorrect

Didn't do his homework last night.

Who didn't do his homework? This sentence lacks a subject.

Correct

Sydney didn't do his homework last night.

Incorrect

I deny.

Deny what? This sentence doesn't express a complete thought.

Correct

I deny the charge against me.

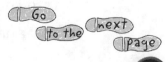

Objects After Preposition

What form of a pronoun do you use after a preposition? Sometimes people write the subject form by mistake.

Rule: Use the object form of a pronoun after a preposition.

Incorrect

They gave the baseball cards to Kevin and I.

Correct

They gave the baseball cards to Kevin and me.

Why does this problem happen? In the sentence above, the preposition is the word *to*. Notice that the words *Kevin and* come before the pronoun. Sometimes this confuses people. The same people who would say *"They gave the baseball cards to me"* will get confused and write *"They gave the baseball cards to Kevin and I."* If you get confused, try saying the sentence without the noun and connecting word (*Kevin and*).

ACTIVITY

Directions Proofread the paragraph below. It contains five errors in grammar. Cross out the error. Write your correction above the error. The first one is done for you.

Sometimes I tell my friends that I am doing nothing, but I'm really doing a lot. When I do nothing, I ~~sat~~ sit on the grass. My body is still but my mind was dreaming. I dream of what I want to be when I grow up. I thought about all the places I want to travel—France, Italy, Hawaii, and China. Sometimes, when I do nothing. I go for a walk I think about things that puzzle me. Why does my little brother always start to cry when I'm just about ready to fall asleep? Why does my best friend Annie get angry with Sally and I when we want to borrow her sweaters? What do monkeys think about. When we look at them in the zoo? Best of all. When I do nothing, I start writing in my mind. I play with ideas I want to develop. I will look into the corners of my mind for new thoughts and ideas. Between you and I, maybe doing nothing is really doing something after all!

LESSON 15   Proofreading

Check Your Punctuation

● ● ● ● ● ● ● ● ● ● ● ● ●

Writers use punctuation marks to show meaning. When you proofread, check that you have punctuated your sentences correctly.

End Marks

End a sentence that makes a statement with a period (.).

The Finger Lakes were names for the Iroquois tribes.

End a sentence that asks a question with a question mark (?).

Have you ever wondered how your town got its name?

End a sentence that expresses great feeling or surprise with an exclamation point.

What a wonderful town this is!

ACTIVITY

Directions Add the correct punctuation mark at the end of each sentence below.

1. Have you heard your cat purr
2. A horse can make sounds like whinny and neigh
3. Some pigs squeal, but dogs say bow-bow
4. That's a really silly thing to say
5. What sounds does your dog make when you play with it
6. Do animals make different sounds in different countries
7. What a surprise that would be
8. I never heard a bird say tweet tweet
9. Can you understand your pet when it talks to you
10. Do you know how to talk to your pet

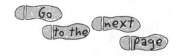
Go to the next page

Underline, Italics, and Quotation Marks

Underline the titles of books, magazines, movies, and full length plays. If you write on a computer, place the title in *italic* type.

> *Harriet the Spy*
> *The Indian in the Cupboard*
> *The Sound of Music*
> *Time for Kids*

Remember to capitalize the first letter of each word in the title except for prepositions and the words *the* and *a*.

Put titles of short works in quotation marks. These include titles of short stories and folktales, poems, magazine articles, one-act plays, and episodes of a TV series.

> "Jack and the Beanstalk"
> "Aladdin and His Magic Lamp"
> "The Owl and the Pussycat"
> "How to Make an Apple Pie"

ACTIVITY

Directions Proofread the paragraph below. It contains five punctuation errors. Cross out each error. Write your correction above the error. The first one is done for you.

James Fenimore Cooper was born in 1789. Have you heard of this great American writer? Cooper's best known work is a set of books called *The Leatherstocking Tales*. These books follow the life of Natty Bumppo. Throughout the books, Natty tries to get away from towns that spring up on the frontier! He wants to live in the wild close to nature. What a life. One book, "The Last of the Mohigans," was made into a movie.

LESSON 16   Proofreading

Check Your Spelling

● ● ● ● ● ● ● ● ● ● ● ● ●

Even the best spellers have some words that trip them up. Here are some commonly misspelled words.

all right	Write *all right* as two words.
already	There is only one *l* in this word.
believe	The letter *i* comes before *e*, except after *c*.
calendar	This word ends with *ar*, not *er*.
definite	This word ends with *ite*, not *ate*.
familiar	Don't forget the second *i* in this word *-iar*.
February	Don't forget the *u* in this word.
forehead	Notice the *e* at the end of the first syllable.
height	This word is an exception. The *e* comes before *i*.
laugh	The letters *gh* spell the sound of *f*.
library	Say this word carefully.
neighbor	The letters *eigh* spell the sound *a*.
Wednesday	This word is very tricky. The letter *d* is silent.

ACTIVITY

Directions **Proofread the paragraph below. It contains ten spelling errors. Cross out each error. Write your correction above the error. The first one is done for you.**

         Wednesday

Last ~~Wensday~~, my neighbors took me to see the animated film *Peter Pan*. It was a cold Febrary, so being inside a movie theater was a definate treat. Since I had read the book *Peter Pan* in the liberry, I was all ready familiar with the story. I had to laff when Peter fought Captain Hook. He flew up to the hight of the mast, while Hook stared helplessly at him Then Peter flew down and brushed his sword against Hook's forehead. Of course, Hook didn't get hurt. Later, I clapped my hands for Tinkerbell. She almost died because people didn't beleve in her. In the end, every thing turned out alright. Wendy returned home, and each calender year, Peter led new children to Never Never Land.

LESSON 17 Proofreading

Check Commonly Confused Words

Here is a list of commonly confused words. Watch for them when you proofread.

affect	a verb meaning "to influence or change"
effect	a noun meaning "a result"
dessert	food served at the end of a meal
desert	a verb meaning "to leave someone or something behind."
	a noun meaning "a dry area where there is little rain"
its	belonging to someone or something
it's	the contraction of *it is*
idol	an image or a statue that some people worship
idle	not busy
lose	a noun that means "to be defeated" or "to come to be without."
loose	an adjective that means "free" or "not attached"
principal	the most important person
principle	a truth or belief
to	a preposition that means "toward" or "on"
too	an adverb that means "also"
two	a noun that is a number

Go to the next page

Measuring Up™ to the New York State Learning Standards

ACTIVITY

Directions Proofread each group of sentences below. There is one error in each item. Cross out the word that is wrong. Write the correct word above it.

1. The ~~principle~~ *Principal* of the school was a good model for us. She taught us principles we should live by.

2. Christina was afraid she would lose the coins. She had too much ~~lose~~ *loose* change in her pocket.

3. The basketball player was an idle to some of the teenagers. He told them to work hard and warned them against being idle.

4. Because it was too hot to stay outside, we ~~saw~~ *went* to *the* movies.

5. The town is closing up its public pools. This is a sure sign that its almost fall.

6. "I won't desert you," said Leroy. "I'll wait until you finish your ~~desert~~ *dessert*."

7. What is the effect of too much exercise? It can effect you by making you tired.

8. We were sad to loose the principal, but she was looking forward to retiring.

9. It's a miracle that we survived a week in the ~~dessert~~ *desert*.

10. We had a serious storm. What was its ~~affect~~ *effect*?

LESSON 18 Proofreading

Use Computer Tools

● ● ● ● ● ● ● ● ● ● ● ● ●

 If you write on a computer, you will find several tools to help you revise. The arrows on the side of your screen help you scroll, or move, the page up and down. The arrows on the bottom of the screen help you move the page from left to right.

ACTIVITY

Directions **Look at the symbols below. On the line below each one, tell what it means.**

_____ _____ _____ _____

Computers help you with revising by making it easy for you to fix your writing. By using a computer, you can do all of the following:

✱ Cut text.

✱ Paste this same text in another place.

✱ Copy text and repeat it somewhere else.

✱ Change the way the type looks.

✱ Make a drawing to include in your writing.

✱ Check your spelling and grammar.

✱ Print your writing.

LESSON 18   Proofreading

ACTIVITY

Directions Look at the computer icons below. Under each icon, tell what you think it means.

_____   _____   _____   _____

_____   _____   _____

ACTIVITY

Directions Think about how using a computer can help make your writing stronger. Write your thoughts on the lines below.

_____

_____

_____

_____

_____

LESSON 19 Publishing

Share Your Writing
· · · · · · · · · · · · · ·

Now you have finished your paper. It's time to share it. Here are
some ideas for sharing your writing.

✿ Read it aloud to your classmates.

✿ Make a book jacket for it and put it on the bulletin board.

✿ Post it on the internet.

✿ Send it to a magazine that publishes student writing.

✿ Make a recording of it.

✿ Make copies of your writing and give them to your friends.

✿ Publish a class magazine containing your writing.

✿ Give it to your parents as a gift.

✿ Visit a kindergarten and read your writing to the children.

ACTIVITY

Directions Work with a group of students to come up with publishing
ideas. Challenge your group to come up with fifteen ideas. Select the most
original idea.

_____

_____

_____

_____

ACTIVITY

Directions Do some research. Find out what magazines publish student
writing. Ask your librarian for help. If you can, gather information from the
internet.

_____

_____

_____

LESSON 20   Publishing

Give a Presentation
• • • • • • • • • • • •

One way to share your writing is to give a presentation. A presentation is a speech or talk before a group of people.

These points will help you give effective presentations.

Prepare yourself.

Ask yourself questions like:
1. Can you pronounce all the hard words?
2. Are you well rested? Do you feel confident? If not, pause and take a deep breath.
3. Are your notes easy-to-read? Are they in order?

How else could you prepare yourself?

_____

Check your equipment.
4. Are you using a poster or chart? Is it large enough to be seen?
5. Is your tape player or CD player ready? Is it set to the right volume?

What other details should you check?

_____

Check yourself while you are speaking.
6. Are you speaking loudly enough?
7. Are you speaking clearly?
8. Are you speaking at the right speed? (Don't go too fast.)

What other things should you think about?

_____

ACTIVITIES

Reading

Be a word hunter. Use a thesaurus or dictionary to find as many synonyms as you can for these words:

silly   **home**   **quick**

_____   _____   _____

_____   _____   _____

_____   _____   _____

Listening

A good way to gather information is to interview members of your community. Choose a topic. Select four people in your community who could give you information about this topic. Write down questions to ask them. With their permission, conduct an interview. Make notes on their answers to your questions.

_____

_____

_____

_____

_____

_____

Go to the next page

ACTIVITIES

Writing

Write a cause and effect paragraph. First choose a topic. Decide what point you would like to make about this topic. Then write a topic sentence. Decide whether your sentence should contain a result or a cause. Write three of more sentences that support this main idea. If you began with a cause, these sentences should give results. If you began with a result, these sentences should give causes. Finally, write a conclusion for your paragraph.

_____

_____

_____

_____

_____

_____

_____

Speaking

Work with a partner. Take turns giving a speech to each other. Make notes on good points and bad points. Are you speaking clearly? Are you going too fast or too slow? Is your voice too loud or too soft? When both of you are finished, talk about how you can improve.

_____

_____

_____

_____

_____

_____

_____

. . . .

What's It All About?

In this chapter, you will learn

✱ how to listen well

✱ how to write a short answer

✱ how to write a longer answer

✱ how your answers will be marked

✱ how to use a time order chain

✱ how to use a cause and effect map

✱ how to use a compare and contrast circle

What Does the Test Look Like?

In this part of the test, you will be doing something a little different. Instead of reading, you will listen to your teacher read a story aloud. Then you will answer questions about it. One question will have you fill out a chart, or graphic organizer. Doing this will show that you can organize your ideas and remember what you've heard. One question asks you to write a short answer. One question asks you to write a longer answer. In this chapter, you are going to practice writing answers to the types of questions you will find on the test.

How Much Time Do You Have?

The test today will last for 60 minutes. Give yourself about 30 minutes to finish this part of the test. Think about how you should divide up your time. Here is one way:

5 minutes	Fill out the chart, or graphic organizer.
5 minutes	Answer the short question.
20 minutes	Answer the long question

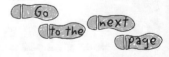

Go to the next page

Things to Remember

1. The story is not in your test booklet.
2. Your teacher will read the story aloud twice.
3. Take notes as you listen the second time.
4. Keep track of time.
5. Write your answers in the test booklet.
6. Take your pick. Print or write in cursive.
7. Make sure your handwriting is neat.

ACTIVITY

Directions See how well you and your classmates listen. Divide into two teams. Each team should pass a message along to each of its team members. The first person on each team whispers the message to the second person. The second person whispers it to the third person. This continues until the message is passed to the last person. The team that passes the message with the fewest changes wins. What did you learn from this activity? Write your thoughts on the lines below.

_____

_____

_____

_____

_____

_____

_____

_____

LESSON 1   How to Listen Well

How well do you listen? When someone gives you directions, do you know what to do? When you hear a story, can you retell the main parts? When you hear information on the radio, can you tell the main ideas? To do well on this part of the test, you must listen well.

Here are some tips for making your listening skills better.

Keys to Success

These strategies will help you be successful when listening to a story. On page 119, you will see how to put these strategies to work.

When you listen,

Pay Attention

This sounds easy, doesn't it. But it's very important and can be tricky. Look at the teacher as the teacher reads aloud. Tune in; make sure you pick up every word. Don't start day dreaming. Don't start thinking about what you are going to do later on. If your mind starts wandering, pull it back to listening to the story. In other words, pay attention.

Think About What You Hear

Don't let the words go in one ear and out the other. Think about what you are hearing. Listen for main ideas. Listen for details. Check yourself. Make sure you follow what is being said.

Take Notes

Write down important ideas. Write down key words. Draw charts or pictures if that helps you remember information. You can look back at your notes later when you answer the questions.

Go to the next page

 Measuring Up™ to the New York State Learning Standards

ACTIVITY

Directions Use the following chart to make notes as you listen to "The Man, the Boy, and the Donkey" by Aesop.

Title: _____ **Author:** _____
Characters
What Happens First
In the Middle
Last
Words and Phrases to Remember

LESSON 2   How to Write a Short Answer

You've listened well. Now you are ready to write answers to questions. Don't get nervous. Take a deep breath. You are going to do fine. The writer Paula Danzinger once said, "My favorite book as a kid was *The Little Engine That Could*. I still go, 'I think I can, I think I can,' when I'm feeling insecure."

Here are some tips that will help you be successful.

Keys to Success

These strategies will help you be successful when you write your response. On pages 122-123, you will put these strategies to work.

When you write,

Answer the Question

Make sure you read the question carefully. What does the question ask you to do? Underline key words in the question. Ask yourself: Does my answer fit this question?

Be Complete

Make sure you have answered the complete question. Sometimes a question asks you to do more than one thing. Ask yourself: Does the question have more than one part? Have I answered each part?

Plan

Think about what you want to say before you start to write. Go back to your notes. Underline details you want to use in your answer.

Be Clear

Write what you think as clearly as possible. Ask yourself: Will readers understand what I mean? Is there any way I can make my meaning clearer?

Go to the next page

LESSON 2   How to Write a Short Answer

Be Organized

Start with a topic sentence that tells your main idea. Then give details supporting your main idea. Ask yourself: Does my first sentence tell my main idea?

Be Specific

Use details from the story in your answer. Use the names of the characters. Remember the words and phrases from that story you wrote in your notes? Quote them, when appropriate, in your writing. Give as many details as you can. Ask yourself: Have I given specific information? Have I given enough information to make my point?

Show Thought

Show that you have thought about the story. What does the theme mean to you? How does it connect with what you know about life? Ask yourself: Is my answer thoughtful?

GUIDE TO READING THE QUESTIONS	● POINTS TO NOTICE

Sample Graphic Organizer Question

❶ 29. In this fable, the man tries to please everyone. Complete the chart below, explaining what he does to please each of these people.

What They Say	What the Man Does to Please Them
❷ A countryman says, "You fools, what is a donkey but to ride upon?"	The man puts the boy on the donkey.
❸ One man says, "See that lazy youngster. He let's his father walk while he rides."	
One woman says, "Shame on that lazy lout to let his poor little son trudge along."	The man pulls the boy up on the donkey to ride with him.
❹ The men say, "Aren't you ashamed of yourselves for overloading that poor donkey of yours—you and your hulking son?"	

Sample Short Answer Question

❺ 30. Explain why the group of men call the son "lazy." Be sure to use details from the story in your answer.

_____

_____

_____

_____

Points to Notice:

❶ To answer this question, think, "What did the man do because this person said this?" Go back and check your notes for help.

❷ See the answer here. Use this as a model for writing your own answer.

❸ Keep the sequence of events in mind. You might find it helpful to go back and check your notes again.

❹ Don't forget to answer this part of the question.

❺ The key word here is *explain*. Make sure you provide reasons to explain this. These reasons must come from the story.

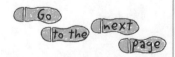
Go to the next page

_____

_____

_____

_____

ACTIVITY

Directions Answer the questions on page 122. Go back to your notes as often as possible. Make sure you provide details and examples from the selections to support your answers.

Check Yourself

Ask yourself

- Did I answer the question that was asked?
- Did I answer all parts of the question?
- Is my answer clear?
- Is my answer well organized?
- Did I use specific details and examples?
- Have I shown that I understood the fable?

Do you know what a good answer looks like? Do you know what teachers will look for when they grade your answer?

Rubrics are the guidelines or benchmarks that will be used to grade your answer. Your answer will be graded on a scale from 0-4, with 4 being the highest grade.

The rubrics below and on the next page are like the ones teachers will use to mark your answer.

Rubric
The Graphic Organizer

4	3	2	1	0
✸ is complete	✸ is brief	✸ may be incomplete	✸ is incomplete	✸ does not answer the question
✸ contains correct information and shows understanding	✸ shows some understanding	✸ may show that the story is not really understood	✸ is inaccurate	✸ is wrong
				✸ does not make sense

The Short Answer

4	3	2	1	0
✱ answers all parts of the question	✱ answers most of the question	✱ answers some of the question	✱ answers only a small part of the question	✱ does not answer the question
✱ shows an understanding of the theme or key elements	✱ addresses some of the key parts of the story	✱ shows understanding of only part of the theme or key elements	✱ misses important parts of the story	✱ is wrong
✱ shows insight	✱ shows a mostly literal understanding	✱ shows some misunderstanding of the story	✱ shows only a little understanding	✱ does not make sense
✱ makes many connections to life and experiences	✱ make some connections	✱ makes few connections to life and experiences	✱ makes no connections	
✱ uses examples from the story to provide good support for the main idea	✱ provides less support	✱ does not contain enough support	✱ may contain details that do not support the main idea	
✱ has no mistakes in grammar, spelling, punctuation, and capitalization	✱ has no mistakes that interfere with meaning in grammar, spelling, capitalization, and punctuation	✱ has some mistakes in grammar, spelling, punctuation, and capitalization	✱ has several mistakes in grammar, spelling, punctuation, and capitalization	

Sample Answers

Question

29. In this fable, the man tries to please everyone. Complete the chart below, explaining what he does to please each of these people.

Answer

What They Say	What the Man Does to Please Them
A countryman says, "You fools, what is a donkey but to ride upon?"	The man puts the boy on the donkey.
One man says, "See that lazy youngster. He let's his father walk while he rides."	**The man makes the boy get off.**
One woman says, "Shame on that lazy lout to let his poor little son trudge along."	The man pulls the boy up on the donkey to ride with him.
The men say, "Aren't you ashamed of yourselves for overloading that poor donkey of yours--you and your hulking son?"	**The man and his son tie the donkey's feet to a pole and carry it on their shoulders.**

Comments

29. This response would be scored as a 3. The story tells us that the man makes the boy get off the donkey, but the answer leaves out an important part. The man then gets on the donkey himself.

Sample Short Answer Question

Question
30. Explain why the group of men call the son "lazy." Be sure to use details from the story in your answer.

Answer

The group of men call the boy lazy because they see him riding on the donkey's back while the man walks. They think that the boy isn't showing respect for his father. They think he should walk while the father rides.

Comments
30. This answer would score a 4. It contains correct information and shows insight. The writer gives the literal reason—they see the boy riding while the man walks. But the writer also interprets this reason. They think this shows disrespect.

ACTIVITY

Directions Use the rubrics to judge your own answers.

LESSON 4 How to Write a Long Answer

The long answer gives you a chance to show what you have learned from the story. It usually asks you to interpret, or show insight and understanding.

Often, there is more than one part to the question. Be sure to answer all parts. Remember, your answer will be graded for grammar, spelling, capitalization, and punctuation.

How long should your answer be? There is no set word length for your answer. Think of it as about 100-175 words. But make sure you have answered the question completely. If it takes you 200 words to do this, that's fine.

You will find a planning page in your test booklet. This page is there to help you. It won't be graded. Use it to brainstorm. Jot down ideas. Draw pictures, if that helps you. Use it to organize your ideas.

Keys to Success

These strategies will help you be successful when you write your answer. On page 130-131, you will put these strategies to work.

When you read

Stick to the Topic

The more you write, the easier it is to lose your topic. Stay focused. Make sure everything you write answers the question. Ask yourself: Did I stick to my topic? Did I let my thoughts wander?

Organize

Before you start writing, plan how you will organize your ideas. Look for key words in the question. For example, does it tell you to explain how characters are alike and how they are different? Then use comparison and contrast to organize your writing. Ask yourself: Is my organization clear?

Connect Ideas

Use words that connect ideas. These are words like *because, since, after, later, first, next,* and *last.* Ask yourself: Did I use words that help readers move from one idea to the next?

Go to the next page

 Measuring Up™ to the New York State Learning Standards

Use Vivid Language

Remember to use vivid adjectives and adverbs when you describe something. Use concrete nouns. Use similes and other figures of speech to make your writing vivid and interesting. Ask yourself: Could I have said this in a more interesting way? Should I use more vivid language?

Keep Your Writing Style Interesting

Use details from the story in your answer. Use the names of the characters. Remember those words and phrases that you wrote in your notes from the story? Quote them, when appropriate, in your writing. Give as many details as you can. Ask yourself: Have I given specific information? Have I given enough information to make my point?

Proofread

Check for grammar mistakes. Catch those spelling errors. Make sure your punctuation and capitalization are correct. Ask yourself: Have I corrected any mistakes in grammar, spelling, punctuation, and capitalization?

GUIDE TO READING THE QUESTIONS

Sample Long Answer

❶ 31. This fable teaches a lesson: *Please all, and you will please none*. Think about the meaning of this **❷** lesson. Then explain how this fable teaches that lesson. In your answer, be sure to:

❸ Put the lesson in your own words.

❹ Give specific examples from the fable.

❺ Check your writing for correct spelling, grammar, capitalization, and punctuation.

_____

_____

_____

_____

_____

_____

_____

_____

_____

_____

_____

_____

❶ Read the moral, or lesson carefully. This is the most important part of the question. In your answer, you have to show that you understand this moral.

❷ Look at the key word *explain*. The question is asking you to explain how the fable teaches the lesson.

❸ This is the first thing you must do in your explanation.

❹ This is the second thing you must do. Go back to your notes to find specific examples.

❺ Don't forget this step. Proofread.

Go to the next page

_____

_____

_____

_____

_____

_____

_____

_____

_____

_____

ACTIVITY

Directions **Write an answer to the question. Plan your writing on a separate piece of paper.**

Self Evaluation

Ask yourself

Did I stick to the topic?

Is my answer well organized?

Did I connect my ideas?

Did I use vivid language?

Is my writing interesting?

Have I proofread my answer?

LESSON 5 How Your Answer Will Be Marked

Teachers will look for the same things in your long answer that they looked for in your short answer. In addition, they will judge your answer using these standards. The rubric below is similar to the one teachers will use to judge your writing.

Rubric
The Long Answer

4	3	2	1	0
✱ keeps to the topic	✱ may contain a few details that do not fit the topic	✱ tries to stay focused on the topic but contains details that do not connect	✱ may contain many details that do not connect to the topic	✱ does not fit the topic
✱ is well organized	✱ is somewhat organized	✱ shows some attempt at organization	✱ shows little or no organization	✱ is not correct
✱ is well written, using vivid language and interesting sentences	✱ is somewhat easy-to-read, using mainly short sentences and basic vocabulary	✱ is not very interesting, using only simple sentences and basic vocabulary	✱ uses only simple words and sentences and contains sentence fragments	

Sample Long Answer

Question

31. This fable teaches a lesson: *Please all, and you will please none.* Think about the meaning of this lesson. Then explain how this fable teaches that lesson. In your answer, be sure to

Put the lesson in your own words.

Give specific examples from the fable.

Check your writing for correct spelling, grammar, capitalization, and punctuation.

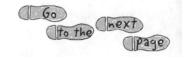
Go to the next page

Measuring Up™ to the New York State Learning Standards

Answer

"The Man, the Boy, and the Donkey" teaches an important lesson. It says that there is no way you can please everyone. If you try to do this, no one will be happy. The only person you can really please is yourself. You need to do what you think is right an stop worrying about what other people think is right. This makes sense to me. When you try to please everyone, you get confused. What makes one person happy makes another person angry. You need to know what you believe and try to do the right thing.

Look at the poor man in this fable. He can't do anything right! First he tries to please one man. He puts his son on the donkey, but he gets yelled at by another man. When he tries to please this man by riding the donkey himself, he gets yelled at by the woman. When he tries to please this woman by having them both ride the donkey, he gets yelled at by another man. Finally, he gets so confused, both he and his son carry the donkey. Then they lose the donkey when it falls over a bridge. No one is happy including the man. He should have done what he believed was right instead of listening to everyone else.

Comments

This answer gets a 4. Look at how complete it is. The answer covers both points of the assignment. The writer puts the lesson in his own words. He also shows what these words mean to him. Then he provides specific examples from the fable to show how the fable teaches this lesson. This answer is thoughtful. The writer ends by giving his own conclusion. He says that the man should have done what he believed was right instead of listening to everyone else.

LESSON 6   Sequence Chain

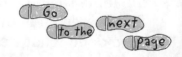

A sequence chain helps you keep track of events. It's a good tool to use when you want to:

* give directions
* follow a recipe
* tell an anecdote
* relate an episode in a person's life
* tell a story
* tell about an event in history

Directions

• • • • • • • • • • •

To complete a sequence chain, follow these directions.

1. Put the event that happens first in the box at the top of the page.
2. Put the event that happens last in the box at the bottom of the page.
3. Choose only important events. Fill in the other boxes with these events.
4. Put the event that happens second in the second box, the event that happens third in the third box, and so on.

Go to the next page

     Measuring Up™ to the New York State Learning Standards

ACTIVITY

Directions Choose one of the following topics or come up with your own:

- how to bake a cake
- how to play a computer game
- how to make a model airplane
- how to play softball
- how to write a book

Use the sequence chain to show the steps.

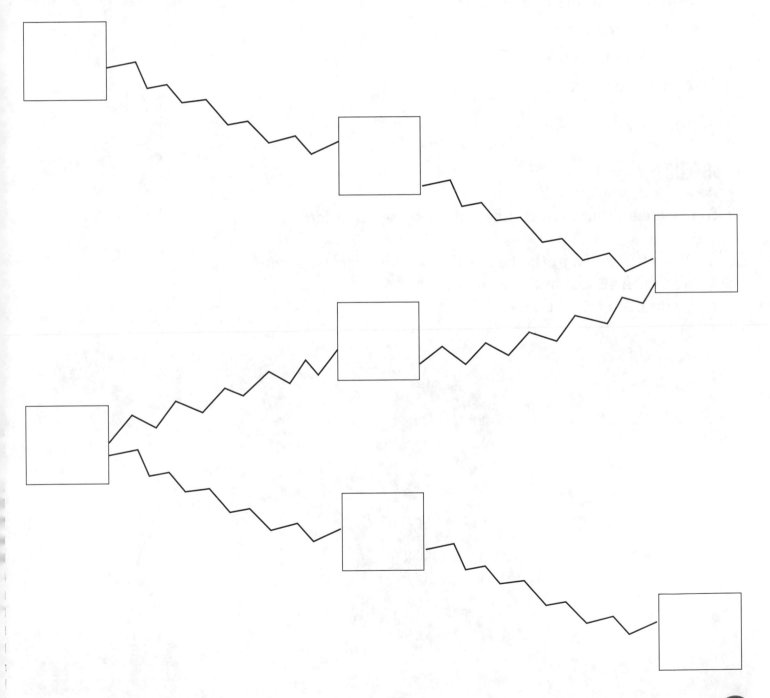

LESSON 7 Cause and Effect Map

A *cause* can make many things happen. An *effect* is the result of the cause. A cause and effect chart is a good tool to use when you want to

* explain why something happened
* tell the causes of an event
* tell the results of an experiment
* give a warning
* explain motives
* make predictions

Directions

● ● ● ● ● ● ● ● ● ● ● ● ●

To use a cause and effect map, follow these directions.

1. Write the cause in the box at the bottom of the diagram.
2. Write the effects in the rings.
3. If you need to, add circles.

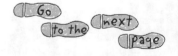
Go to the next page

LESSON 7 Cause and Effect Map

ACTIVITY

Directions What would happen if the school day was made one hour longer? Use the cause and effect map to record your ideas about this topic.

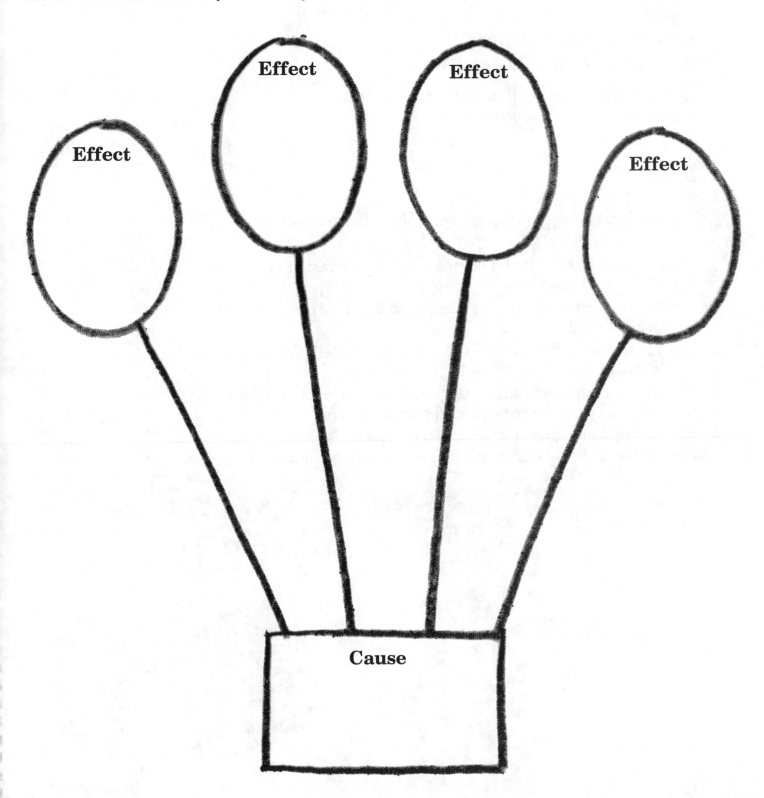

LESSON 8   Compare and Contrast Circles

When you compare, you show how things are alike. When you contrast, you show how they are different. Compare and contrast circles help you

* describe two or more people
* describe two or more places
* persuade someone that one choice is better (or worse) than another

Directions

• • • • • • • • • • •

To use compare and contrast circles, follow these directions.

1. Write the first item being compared and contrasted on top of the circle at the left.
2. Write the second item being compared and contrasted on top of the circle at the right.
3. Fill in the unshaded part of the circle on the left. List words and phrases that describe only the first item.
4. Fill in the unshaded part of the circle on the right. List words and phrases that describe only the second item.
5. Fill in the shaded part where the circles overlap with words and phrases that describe both the first and second item.

Go to the next page

       Measuring Up™ to the New York State Learning Standards

LESSON 8 Compare and Contrast Circles

ACTIVITY

Directions Choose one of the following topics or pick your own:

- two brands of potato chips
- two makes of cars
- two stores selling pizza
- two music groups
- two actors

Jot down your thoughts about how they are the same and how they are different. Use the compare and contrast circles to organize your ideas.

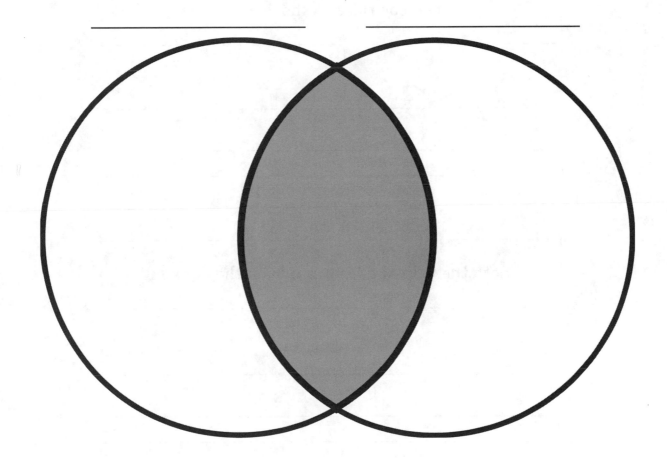

Copying is illegal.

You have learned a lot about graphic organizers. Here is a sample of a test question using a graphic organizer.

29.   The sequence chain below contains some of the events from "The Man, the Boy, and the Donkey." Fill in the missing events.

A man and his son are walking to the market.

The boy rides on the donkey.

_____

Both the man and his son ride on the donkey.

_____

The donkey falls over the bridge and drowns.

LESSON 10 Independent Practice

Directions
Now you will listen to another story. It is a folktale from India called "How Sun, Moon, and Wind Went Out to Dinner." Write notes below as you listen to the tale the second time.

Notes

_____

_____

_____

_____

_____

_____

_____

_____

_____

_____

_____

_____

_____

_____

_____

_____

_____

_____

_____

_____

_____

Go On

29. Use details from the story to show how Sun and Wind
    are similar to each other and how they are different from Moon.

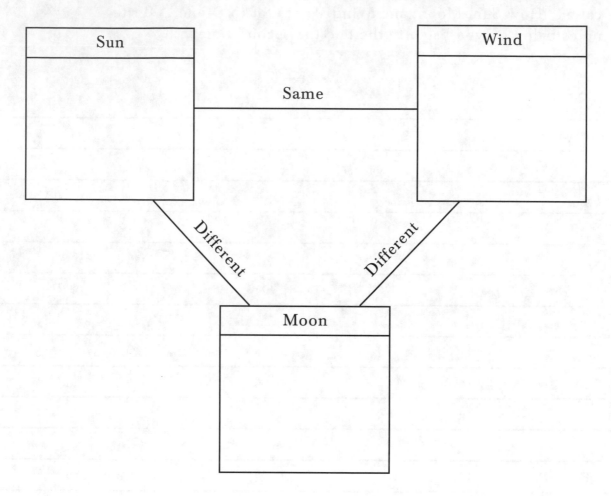

| Sun | | Wind |

Same

Different   Different

Moon

30. Explain why Moon's light is "so soft and cool and beautiful."
    Use details from the folktale in your answer.

_____

_____

_____

_____

_____

Go On

31. Which lesson do you learn from this folktale?
    Circle your answer.

    It's better to think of yourself first.

    It's better to think of other people first.

Explain how this folktale helps teach this lesson.
In your answer, be sure to

  • tell what each sister is like

  • tell what each of the sisters does

  • tell what happens to each of the sisters

Check your writing for correct grammar, spelling,
punctuation, and capitalization.

_____

_____

_____

_____

_____

_____

_____

_____

_____

_____

_____

_____

ACTIVITIES

Reading

Find out more information about Aesop, a storyteller from ancient Greece. Use at least three different sources to get details. Write your notes on the lines below. Share your findings with your classmates.

_____

_____

_____

_____

_____

Listening

Folktales are often passed down orally from one generation to another. Talk to four adults in your community. Ask them to tell you a folktale they remember vividly. Write notes about these folktales below. Share your findings with your classmates.

_____

_____

_____

_____

_____

Go to the next page

ACTIVITIES

Writing

The moral of Aesop's folktale "The Man, the Boy, and the Donkey" is: Please all, and you will please none. Write your own folktale to support this lesson. First brainstorm ideas for your tale. Decide on your animal characters. After writing your first draft, go back and revise your tale. Finally proofread it, checking for mistakes in grammar, spelling, capitalization, and punctuation. Jot down your plan for your tale on the lines below.

_____

_____

_____

_____

_____

_____

_____

Speaking

Go to the library and look through books of folktales. Find one you really like. Practice reading it aloud. Change your voice for each of the characters. Make sure you know how to pronounce each of the words. When you feel comfortable, read the folktale aloud to your classmates. On the lines below, write down how well you think you did.

_____

_____

_____

_____

_____

_____

Chapter 5 WRITING A COMPOSITION

What's It All About?

In this chapter, you will learn

* how to write a composition
* how your answer will be marked
* how to write to inform
* how to write a response to literature
* how to write critically

What Does the Test Look Like?

It's still Day 2 of the test. You have just finished writing responses to listening to a selection. Now you will read a writing prompt and write a composition.

No doubt, you have written many compositions before. This is your chance to show how well you can write and think. It is your chance to express your thoughts

How Much Time Do You Have?

Did you take 30 minutes to write your responses to the listening selection? If so, you have 30 minutes left to finish this part of the test. If you took a little bit longer or a little bit less time, you need to adjust your time.

Here's one way you can divide up your time.

Prewrite	5 minutes
Draft	15 minutes
Revise	5 minutes
Proofread	5 minutes

Go to the next page

ACTIVITY

Directions Think about all the things you have learned about writing this year. Review the compositions in your writing portfolio. Then answer these questions.

1. How has my writing improved so far this year?_____

_____

_____

_____

_____

_____

2. What is the best piece of writing I did this year?
   What made it so good?

_____

_____

_____

_____

_____

_____

3. What can I do to continue to grow as a writer?_____

_____

_____

_____

_____

_____

LESSON 1   How to Write a Composition

Do you know the writer Laurence Yep? You may have read his book *Dragonwings*. Or you may have read *Child of the Owl*. Laurence Yep once wrote:

> I think of writing as a way of seeing. It's a way of bringing out the specialness of ordinary things.

Writing a composition is doing just this. It is letting your readers know why a topic is important or interesting.

A composition has three parts:

* an opening paragraph
* two or more paragraphs that develop the idea
* a closing paragraph

Here are some tips for writing good compositions.

Keys to Success

These strategies will help you be successful when you write your composition. On pages 151-158, you will see how to put these strategies to work.

When you write, look for

An Interesting Beginning

Begin your composition with a strong opening paragraph. This paragraph should tell your most important idea about the topic. It is your chance to put your best foot forward and grab your readers' attention. You might do this by asking a question or telling a little story. You might do it by including a quotation or by including astounding facts. Ask yourself: Does my opening paragraph tell my main idea? Will it grab my readers' interest?

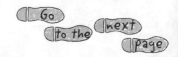
Go to the next page

A Strong Body

The body of your composition consists of the two or more paragraphs you write to develop your main idea. Think of the body as the filling in your sandwich. It is the meat or fish or peanut butter and jelly that comes between the two slices of bread. Remember that a paragraph is a group of sentences that develops one point. Each paragraph in the body of your composition develops a different point that supports your main idea. Ask yourself: Does the body of my composition make points that back up my main idea? Does each paragraph make a different point?

A Forceful Conclusion

Don't let your composition dribble to an end. End with a punch. Write a forceful conclusion that reinforces your main idea and goes a little beyond it. You might recommend action or tell what special meaning something has for you. You might tell why you think this topic is important. Ask yourself: Does my conclusion restate my main idea? Does it bring the ideas to a close in a powerful way?

The Writing Process

Follow the steps of the writing process. Remember to take time to plan and brainstorm ideas. Revise your writing and proofread it to correct any errors. Remember, though, that this is a timed test. You will not have as much time as you might like to revise. In addition, you must keep your paper neat and legible.

ACTIVITY

Directions Write a strong beginning sentence for a composition about each of the following topics.

1. magic tricks _____

_____

2. computer games _____

_____

3. shopping malls _____

_____

4. playing soccer _____

_____

Go to the next page

LESSON 1   How to Write a Composition

GUIDE TO READING THE QUESTION

● POINTS TO NOTICE

Sample

❶ 32. Sometimes a team can do things that one person cannot do alone. Write about a time when you learned **❷** the importance of teamwork, or when someone you **❸** know did. In your story, be sure to include

     ❹ ✱ what you or someone else learned

     ✱ when the lesson was learned

     ✱ what happened

     ❺ ✱ specific details and examples

❻ Proofread your writing to correct errors in grammar, spelling, punctuation, and capitalization.

❶ This question asks you to tell about an event.

❷ The person you write about may be yourself or someone you know. This is not a made-up story. It is about someone from real life.

❸ The event is someone learning the importance of teamwork.

❹ There are three points you must include in your story.

❺ Remember to be specific, not vague. Include actual details and examples from the event.

❻ Don't forget this important step. Proofread!

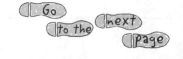

Go to the next page

GUIDE FOR WRITING

Prewriting

1. Choose the person you are going to write about. Will it be you or someone else?

_____

2. Fill out the chart below.

Learning About Teamwork

What happened? _____

_____

Who were the people involved? _____

_____

When did this happen?_____

_____

Where did it happen? _____

_____

What caused this event?_____

_____

What lesson was learned from it? _____

_____

Why is this lesson important? _____

_____

Go to the next page

3. Time order is a good way to organize events.
   Fill out the sequence chain below.

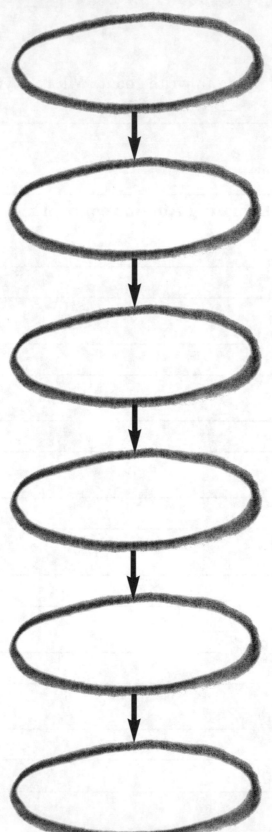

Drafting

4. Write the first draft of your topic sentence for your story.
   Remember to make this sentence so interesting it will
   grab your readers' attention.

_____

_____

_____

_____

_____

5. Look back at the writing prompt. Make sure you understand
   what it is asking you to do. Now write the first draft of your
   opening paragraph.

_____

_____

_____

_____

_____

_____

_____

_____

_____

_____

_____

_____

_____

6. Write two or three paragraphs that develop your main idea.
   Remember to start a new paragraph when you make a new point.

_____

_____

_____

_____

_____

_____

_____

_____

_____

_____

_____

_____

_____

_____

_____

_____

7. Write a forceful conclusion for your story.

_____

_____

_____

_____

_____

_____

Go to the next page

Revising

8. Reread your opening paragraph. Make sure you have a strong beginning. Answer these questions.

   ✱ Does my topic sentence tell my main idea?
     How could I make it better?

   _____

   ✱ Will this paragraph make readers want to read more?
     How could I make it better?

   _____

   Revise your opening paragraph to make it stronger.

9. Make sure the paragraphs in the body of your story support your main idea. Answer these questions.

   ✱ Does all of the information support the main idea?
     If not, what should I do?

   _____

   ✱ Have I begun a new paragraph for each point?
     If not, what should I do?

   _____

   Revise the paragraphs in the body of your story so that they support the main idea.

10. Make sure your body paragraphs contain specific details and examples. Answer these questions.

   ✱ Are my points clear? Have I said exactly what I wanted to say? If not, what should I do?

   _____

   ✱ Are my details and examples specific? If not, what should I do?

   _____

   ✱ Have I used enough details and examples? If not, what should I do?

   _____

   Revise the body of your story to make it more specific.

11. Make sure you end with a forceful conclusion. Ask yourself these questions.

   ✱ Have I ended with a punch? If not, what should I do?

   _____

   ✱ Does my conclusion make my main idea even stronger? If not, what should I do?

   _____

12. Make sure your writing style is interesting. Answer these questions.

   ✱ Have I varied the way my sentences begin? If not, what should I do?

   _____

Have I varied the length of my sentences?
If not, what should I do?

_____

Have I used the same words over and over again?
If so, which words should I change?

_____

Have I used weak words rather than strong words?
If so, which words should I change?

_____

Revise your writing to make it more interesting.

Proofread

13. Correct any errors in grammar. Answer these questions.

Have I used the correct tense of verbs?
If not, which verbs do I need to fix?

_____

Does my story contain sentence fragments?
If it does, which sentences do I need to fix?

_____

Does my story contain any other errors in grammar?
If so, how can I correct them?

_____

Proofread your story again, correcting all grammar errors.

14. Correct any errors in spelling, punctuation, and capitalization. Answer these questions.

   ✱ Does my story contain any spelling errors? If so, which words do I need to correct?

_____

   ✱ Does my story contain any punctuation errors? If so, what punctuation do I need to correct?

_____

   ✱ Does my story contain any capitalization errors? If so, what items do I need to fix?

_____

Proofread your story again, correcting all errors.

LESSON 2   How Your Answer Will Be Marked

Teachers will use a scale of 0-3 to grade your answer. A 3 is the best response. A 0 means three things: (1) The response is completely incorrect, (2) the response doesn't answer the question, and (3) the response doesn't make sense. Think positively! Plan on writing a response that gets a 3. What does your story have to look like to receive a 3? Here is a rubric, or guide. It is similar to the one the teacher will use to mark the test. Correct spelling, punctuation, and capitalization count. Your answer will be graded for these, too.

Rubric

The response

3	2	1
answers every part of the question	✻ answers some parts of the question	✻ answers only a few parts of the question
makes connections to life	✻ makes some connections to life	✻ makes only a few connections to life
supports the main idea with specific details	✻ uses specific details, but may not show how they support the main idea	✻ contains only a few specific details
has enough details to support the main idea	✻ is brief	✻ is too brief
connects the details so that they hold together	✻ tries to connect the details but they may not all hold together	✻ shows little connection between details
is interesting and easy to read	✻ is somewhat interesting and easy-to-read	✻ is not very interesting or easy-to-read
uses varied sentences and vocabulary	✻ uses mostly simple sentences and vocabulary	✻ uses only simple sentences and vocabulary

Sample Answer

I awoke with a start. My cat's cries rang out in the night. Where was Cressie? All I could hear was her crying pitifully. I grabbed a flashlight and ran outside to try to find her. Her crying grew more panicked. Where could she be? I followed the sound of her crying to an old, empty well and beamed my flashlight down it. There she was, crouched on a shelf about halfway down. Her golden eyes shone as she looked to me for help. But I was up at the top of the well, alone, while she was down there. My heart sank because I didn't know how to get to her. Then I noticed my parents running toward me. Other parents and children came streaming from their houses. They had heard her crying, too. I breathed a sigh of relief. Alone, I wasn't sure I could save my cat. Working as a team, I was sure we could.

Teamwork means that people work together to help each other. That night I saw the people in my neighborhood pull together with only one goal in mind—to save my cat. Mrs. Schuster organized them. She told each person what to do. First she sent her daughter to call the fire department. Then she sent some children to get rope and a bowl of food. A couple of grownups went to find wooden boards.

Teamwork also means planning together. We talked over Mrs. Schuster's plan. She wanted to send food down to Cressie to quiet her down while we waited for the fire department, but Michael had another idea. "Let's make a platform and use the food as bait," he said. We all agreed. Part of the group worked together to make a cradle from the rope. Others cut the wooden boards. Finally, we sent food down to Cressie on the platform. Hungry and scared, she sniffed the air and walked right onto the plank. Then the men hauled her up.

Teamwork saved my cat. Before the fire truck came, Cressie was in the house, sitting on my bed and snuggling under the covers. The fire captain told me I had done a great job. "It wasn't just me," I said. "We did it together. Teamwork saved the day!"

Go to the next page

ACTIVITY

Directions Form a group of three or four students.
Talk about this sample response. Ask:

- **Is it interesting?**
- **Is it well written?**
- **Does it include specific information that supports the main idea?**
- **Is the conclusion strong?**

Write your comments on the lines below. Then use the rubric to decide on a grade for it. Share the reasons for your grade with your classmates.

_____

_____

_____

_____

_____

_____

_____

_____

_____

LESSON 3   Writing to Inform

Remember This!

● ● ● ● ● ● ● ● ● ● ● ● ● ●

Tell how you learned to do something, like ride a bike or ice skate.

Show why honesty is the best policy.

Explain how ice skating and in-line skating are the same and how they are different.

Discuss the things you learned at computer camp.

When you write to inform, you give information about a topic. You provide facts, data, and ideas about this subject. Explanations, reports, directions—these are all types of writing that informs.

Notice the words in boldface in the writing prompts above. These help you see that you are going to write to give information. Here are some other writing prompts that ask you to write to give information.

Give directions telling how to make a piñata.

Define the word "honesty."

Identify the causes for the Civil War.

Tell why plants are green.

Describe the way the trees change as the season changes from summer to fall.

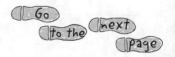

What You Should Know About Writing to Inform

❋ Informative writing contains information—data, facts, ideas, and reasons.

❋ This information may come from what you already know. It may also come from what you learn through reading, listening, and viewing.

❋ It is important to make sure that the information you include is accurate, or correct.

❋ Information may take the form of graphs, charts, or maps.

❋ The information backs up, or supports, the main idea.

❋ You may interpret information, or tell what you think it means.

ACTIVITY

Directions Write a prompt that asks for information. Team up with a partner. Exchange your prompts. You should write in response to your partner's prompt. Your partner should write in response to your prompt.

_____

_____

_____

_____

_____

_____

LESSON 4 Writing in Response to Literature

TIME OUT FOR SKILLS

Remember This!
● ● ● ● ● ● ● ● ● ● ● ● ●

Describe the setting of the story.

Tell whether you found the images in the poem effective.

Express your reaction to the end of the story.

Compare and contrast the two characters.

When you write in response to literature, you interpret what you read. You also evaluate it, or tell how good or effective you think it is. You think about literary elements—plot, character, setting, and theme—and tell how they added to your enjoyment of the story.

Look at the prompts above. They ask you to write in response to literature. Notice the words printed in boldface.

Here are some additional prompts that ask you to write in response to literature.

Interpret the meaning of the last lines of the poem.

Describe the behavior of the main character.

Identify the similes and metaphors.

Make connections between the theme of the story and your own life.

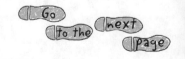
Go to the next page

What You Should Know About Writing in Response to Literature

* When you write in response to literature, you show that you understand the theme, setting, plot, and character.

* In your response, you connect what you have read with your own experience and life.

* You present personal opinions, and you back up these opinions with details from the literature.

* You compare and contrast elements of the selection and of one or more selections.

* You show why what you have read is important or meaningful to you.

ACTIVITY

Directions When we read short stories or novels, we get to know the characters so well that they almost seem like friends. Choose a character from a book you have read. Freewrite for five minutes, telling how this character is like or unlike one of your friends.

_____

_____

_____

_____

_____

_____

Remember This!

• • • • • • • • • • • • • •

Determine whether the book is well written or not.

Decide whether the poet uses language effectively or not.

Evaluate the likelihood of the outcome of the story.

Analyze the use of images in the poem.

When you write critically, you make a judgment about the merit of something. You determine whether or not you find something effective or good.

Look at the boldface words in the prompts above. They help you see that the prompt is asking you to write critically.

Below are some additional prompts that ask for a critical response.

Judge whether or not you found the setting believable.

Determine how the author created suspense in the story.

Evaluate the plot of the mystery.

Analyze the motives of the characters.

 Measuring Up™ to the New York State Learning Standards

What You Should Know About Writing Critically

✱ Notice the word critic in critically. When you write critically, you write like a critic.

✱ When you write critically, you may tell *why* you think something works.

✱ When you write critically, you may tell *whether* you think something works.

✱ When you write critically, you may *compare* the merit of two or more things.

✱ When you write critically, you *support* your judgment with details and examples from the text.

ACTIVITY

Directions A book review is a type of critical writing. Write a review of a book you have recently read. In your review be sure to tell

- **what you liked best about the book**
- **what you thought could be improved or made better**
- **whether or not you think your friends would enjoy the book**

_____

_____

_____

_____

_____

_____

LESSON 6   Apply to the Test

You've been learning a lot about different types of responses. Here are examples of writing prompts on tests.

Sample Writing to Inform Prompt

Write about two people you know who have taught you an important lesson in life. In your composition, be sure to include

* who the people are

* how they taught you a lesson

* what the lesson means to you

* specific details and examples

Proofread your composition to correct spelling, punctuation, capitalization, and grammar.

Sample Literary Response Prompt

Choose two poems that create a vivid picture of winter. Write a composition comparing and contrasting these poems. In your composition, be sure to include

* what the poems are

* who the authors are

* how each poem makes you feel about winter

* specific details and examples

Proofread your composition to correct any grammar, spelling, punctuation, and capitalization errors.

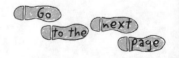
Go to the next page

Sample Writing Critically Response

Sometimes you hear good things about a book but are disappointed when you read it. Write a composition telling why you didn't like a book you read as much as you thought you would. In your composition, be sure to include

- ✱ the title and author of the book
- ✱ what you first heard about it that made you want to read it
- ✱ why it didn't live up to your expectations
- ✱ specific details and examples

Proofread your composition to correct any grammar, spelling, punctuation, and capitalization errors.

ACTIVITY
Directions Choose one of the writing prompts and write your response.

_____

_____

_____

_____

_____

_____

_____

_____

_____

_____

_____

Planning Page

Use this page to brainstorm ideas and plan your writing.

_____

_____

_____

_____

_____

_____

_____

_____

_____

_____

_____

_____

_____

_____

_____

_____

_____

_____

_____

_____

_____

_____

_____

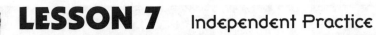

Persistence means "keeping on doing something even when there are roadblocks in your way." Write about a time when you or a person you know learned about the importance of persistence. In your story be sure to include

* what happened

* what this person learned from this event

* why learning this was important

* specific details and examples

Proofread your story to correct any errors in grammar, spelling, capitalization, or punctuation.

_____

_____

_____

_____

_____

_____

_____

_____

_____

_____

_____

ACTIVITIES

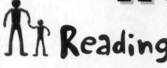 **Reading**

Find an example of an article written to inform. A good place to find articles is *Time for Kids* or *Scholastic News* or *Weekly Reader*. Write a summary of the news article on the lines below.

_____

_____

_____

_____

_____

Listening

Answering the question that was asked is a difficult skill. It is very easy to start answering the question and lose your way and slip off track. Listen to an interview on the radio or television. How many times does the person being interviewed answer the exact question that was asked? How many times does the person end up answering a different question altogether? Report your findings to your classmates.

_____

_____

_____

_____

_____

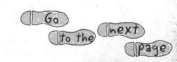

Measuring Up™ to the New York State Learning Standards

ACTIVITIES

 Writing

Keeping a literature log or journal helps you keep track of your response to the books and other stories you have read. If you are not already keeping a journal, start one now. Write in it every day. Jot down all of your thoughts about what you have read. Write the title for your journal on the lines below.

_____

_____

_____

_____

_____

_____

Speaking

Think of a career you would like to learn more about. Prepare a list of questions to ask someone in this profession. Rehearse asking your questions. Then set up an interview and interview this person.

_____

_____

_____

_____

_____

Chapter 6 WRITING IN RESPONSE TO READING

What's It All About?

In this chapter, you will learn

* how to connect information from one selection to another
* how to write a short answer
* how to write a long answer
* how your answer will be marked
* how to proofread

What Does the Test Look Like?

This is the last day of the test. You will read two selections, both about the same topic. After you read the first article, you will fill out a chart and write a short response to a question. Then you will read the second article and write a short response to a question about it. Finally, you will write a long response to a question connecting both the selections.

Wow! That's a lot to do. However, you are already way ahead of the game. You've practiced writing short responses and long responses. Now you are going to learn how to connect selections and practice writing some more.

How Much Time Do You Have?

This part of the test lasts for 60 minutes. Plan how you want to divide up your time. One way to do it is like this.

Read the first selection	15 minutes
Fill out the graphic organizer	5 minutes
Write your short response	5 minutes
Read the second selection	10 minutes
Write your short response	5 minutes
Write your long response	20 minutes

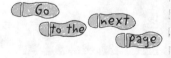

Things to Remember

1. The selections are in your test booklet.
2. You can write on the page with the selection. You might want to underline or highlight important information.
3. You can go back to the selection as often as you like when you write your answer.
4. Keep track of time.
5. Write your answers in the test booklet.
6. You can print or write in cursive. It's your choice.
7. Make sure your handwriting is easy to read.

ACTIVITY

Directions Here's a little activity to get you started. You have probably read a lot about heroes. They may be folk heroes from folktales and legends, heroes from Greek and Roman myths or myths from other cultures, or heroes from real life. Freewrite for five minutes about a hero.

_____

_____

_____

_____

_____

_____

_____

_____

_____

_____

Every time you read about a topic you learn something new. By connecting all of the information, you begin to form a pretty complete picture. For example, imagine you saw the movie *Pocahontas*. You got excited by her story and wanted to learn more about her. First you went to the encyclopedia where you learned facts about her life. Then you read more about her in your history book. Finally, you read Longfellow's poem about her. Every time you read something new, you compared the new information against what you already knew.

Keys to Success

These strategies will help you be successful when you read two selections. You will put these strategies to work on page 177.

When you read,

Connect Details

Connect details you learn from one source with details you learn from another source. Compare the information. See if the details in one source support the details in another source. See if there are any differences.

Connect Main Ideas

Different stories or sources might take different positions or have different opinions about the same topic. Find the main idea in each selection. See if they agree. If they don't, see which you agree with.

Connect Text Types

Different forms of writing present information in different ways. A narrative gives you a story and often helps you understand a person's thoughts and feelings. Informational writing is more likely to give you a lot of facts and details and figures. Critical writing is likely to make judgments and tell you the merit of something. When you read different text types, remember the purpose of each.

READING GUIDE   ● **GUIDED QUESTIONS**

Directions You are going to read an article called "Grandma Moses: Making the Most of Life" and an encyclopedia entry about Grandma Moses. Use the questions and the comments on the side to guide you.

Grandma Moses, veteran master of painting in the primitive style, takes a nostalgic look at *Christmas at Home*, from a collection of her paintings on display at a show in New York City.

❶ Grandma Moses:
Making the Most of Life

By Pat McCarthy

❷ The tiny gray-haired woman walked briskly up the sidewalk to her house in Eagle Bridge, New York. The door flew open. "Grandma," cried

This artist's paintings make people feel good.

her daughter-in-law Dorothy, "if you had been here, you could have sold all your paintings! There was a man here looking for them, and he will be back in the morning to see them." Dorothy had told the man that Grandma had about ten paintings.

❸ Grandma hardly slept that night. She got up early and found nine pictures. She cut one big painting in half and put it in two frames so there would be ten. "I did it so it wouldn't get Dorothy in the doghouse," she explained later.

❹ Grandma's real name was Anna Mary Robertson Moses. She didn't become serious about painting until she was in her mid-seventies. She was almost eighty when she sold those first paintings in 1938. The man who bought them was Louis J. Caldor, an art collector.

❶ What does this title make you think the article will tell you about Grandma Moses?

❷ What do you learn about Grandma Moses in this paragraph?

❸ Why did Grandma Moses cut a painting in half? What does this tell you about her?

❹ What three facts do you learn about Grandma Moses in this paragraph?

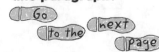
Go to the next page

5 He helped to get Grandma's pictures into a show of many artists' work at a New York City museum. Then, in 1940, an art gallery held a show of Grandma's pictures all by themselves. But Grandma didn't go to either show. She said she had already seen the paintings!

6 A month later, Grandma did go to New York. Gimbels' department store invited her to see a display of her pictures at its Thanksgiving festival. Here, people got to know Grandma Moses and her art. Grandma charmed everyone with her lively personality. Her paintings of happy times in the country made people feel good about the world.

7 As years passed, people became even more interested in Grandma and her work. In 1955, the famous news reporter Edward R. Murrow invited her to be on his TV show, *See It Now*.

8 On the program, people watched Grandma paint a picture at her house. She sat at her old tip-up table and painted on Masonite, a thin hard board. Grandma started with the sky, then painted the hills, trees, buildings, and people. "I like to paint old-timey things," she said. "I like pretty things the best."

5 What inference do you make about Grandma Moses based on her actions?

6 In this paragraph you learn more about her paintings. What were her paintings like?

7 How many years have passed since Grandma Moses sold her first painting?

8 What two other details do you learn about Grandma Moses's painting in this paragraph?

Ready with brush, Grandma Moses mixes colors in her palette, a top off a jelly jar. She spreads papers over table while she works.

Go to the next page

9 Her work is called primitive[1] art, a style of art that is simple and clear. Like Grandma, many primitive artists have not had formal training. But Grandma used her memory, and studied the color of the world outside. This helped her add true-to-life details to her paintings. They show activities such as catching the Thanksgiving turkey, ice-skating, and bringing in the maple sap.

Grandma lived to be 101 and was always active. In the last year of her life, she painted twenty-five pictures.

10 In a book she wrote about herself, Grandma said, "I look back on my life like a good day's work: it was done and I feel satisfied with it. I was happy and contented. . . and made the best out of what life offered." By making the best of her life, Grandma made people happy with her paintings.

---

[1] **primitive:** very simple and basic; unschooled

9 Use the footnote to help you define the word *primitive*. Why do you think this type of art is called "primitive"?

10 Notice that this article contains the exact words of Grandma Moses. What connection do you see between her words and the title?

from Scholastic Encyclopedia of Women in the United States

Grandma Moses   ANNA MARY ROBERTSON MOSES

| born 1860 - died 1961 |
| **PAINTER** |

11 Grandma Moses was over 70 years old when she displayed her paintings in a drugstore window in Hoosick Falls, New York. By the time she died at age 101, people throughout the United State and Europe knew her work.

Anna Mary Robertson grew up on a farm in Washington County, New York. After marrying Thomas Moses in 1887, she had little time left for the art she enjoyed as a child. The Moseses became dairy farmers in Virginia and later New York and raised five children. Anna Mary sometimes still embroidered[1] pictures.

---

[1] **embroidered:** made a picture or design on a cloth using thread

11 The first article opened by telling a little story. This article opens by relating facts. What facts do you learn about Grandma Moses in the first two paragraphs? Think about answers to the 5Ws and H questions.

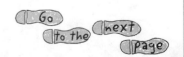
Go to the next page

⑫ Thomas died in 1927. The Moses' eldest son took over the farm, and Grandma Moses now had more time for her embroidery. Then she got arthritis[2] and had to give up her thread-and-yarn pictures. She started painting pictures instead, using house paint and old canvas. In 1939, art collector Louis Caldor saw Moses's paintings exhibited at the drugstore, visited her farm, and bought 15 of her paintings. In October 1939, three of those paintings were included in a show at the Museum of Modern Art in New York City. People loved her work.

⑬ Grandma Moses had her first one-woman show in 1940, when she was 80 years old, at New York City's Galerie St. Etienne. It was the first of 150 solo shows. Her work was also in 100 national and international group shows. Grandma Moses painted around 2,000 pictures, mostly rural[3] landscapes or scenes from her childhood, such as "Catching the Thanksgiving Turkey" (1943), "In Harvest Time" (1943), "Snowballing" (1946), and "The Quilting Bee" (1950). Her paintings have a simple, colorful, childlike quality that is now known as American primitive.

---

[2] **arthritis:** a painful disease that makes people's joints swell
[3] **rural:** having to do with the country or farming

⑫ What fact do you learn in this paragraph that seems to disagree with a fact you learned in the first article? What could account for the difference? How could you find out more about this?

⑬ The first article ended by telling you about the thoughts of Grandma Moses. How does this article end?

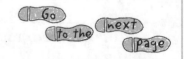

Go to the next page

ACTIVITY

Directions Answer the following questions about both articles.

1. Which article told you more about what Grandma Moses was like and showed you her thoughts and feelings? Give details or examples from the articles to support your answer.

_____

_____

2. Which article gave you more facts, figures, and other data? Give details or examples from the articles to support your answer.

_____

_____

3. How did the pictures and captions in both articles help you learn more about Grandma Moses? Give details or examples from the articles to support your answer.

_____

_____

4. Which statement best expresses the main idea of the first article? Circle the letter of your answer.
   a. Grandma Moses was a good painter.
   b. Grandma Moses made the most out of what life offered her.
   c. Grandma Moses sold many paintings.

5. Which statement best expresses the main idea of the second article? Circle the letter of your answer.
   a. Grandma Moses is a well known American painter who painted simple, colorful paintings of rural scenes.
   b. Grandma Moses gave up embroidery when she got arthritis.
   c. Grandma Moses lived on a farm and raised five children.

ACTIVITY

Directions Did you get a fuller picture of Grandma Moses by reading both articles instead of just one? Explain your answer, using examples and details from both articles.

_____

_____

LESSON 2   How to Write a Short Answer

You already know how to do this. You wrote short answers to the selection you listened to your teacher read. Let's review a bit and practice writing answers to questions about two linked selections.

Keys to Success

These strategies will help you be successful when you write about what you read. On pages 183-189, you will see how to put these strategies to work.

When you write,

Read Directions

The writing prompt, or question, is very important. Read it carefully. Ask yourself: Am I sure I understand what to do?

Go Back to the Selection

Once you understand the question, go back to the selection. Skim it, or reread it quickly, to make sure you understand the points it makes. Scan it, or let your eyes pass quickly over it, to find facts. Ask yourself: Do I need to read the selection again? Do I need to skim it or scan it?

Be Specific

Include specific details and examples from the selection in your answer. Remember to put quotation marks around exact quotations from the selection. Ask yourself: Have I included specific details and examples? Have I included enough details and examples?

Show That You Have Thought About the Selection

You read not only for facts but also for meaning. Make sure your answer shows that you understand the meaning of the selection. Ask yourself: Is my writing thoughtful?

Plan Your Time

Remember that you have sixty minutes to complete this part of the test. Plan your time well so that you can finish the test. The teacher will warn you when your time is almost up. Ask yourself: How much time do I have left?

LESSON 2   How to Write a Short Answer

GUIDE TO READING THE SELECTIONS AND THE QUESTIONS

● **POINTS TO NOTICE**

Directions You are going to read two articles. One is called "The Apple-Seed Man" and the other is called "Arbor Day Celebrates Our Love of Trees." Use the comments and questions on the side to guide your reading.

1

The Apple-Seed Man
by Paula Appling

1 Do you know someone from folktales who might be called "The Apple-Seed Man"? Who do you think this story might be about?

2 Imagine sleeping on a bed of earth with the sky as your roof. Imagine birds and wolves and snakes as your only companions for weeks. Imagine eating nuts and berries and roots that you've freshly harvested and prepared.

John Chapman planted thousands of apple trees as America moved west.

2 Connect these details to your own life. What would it be like to do these things?

3 John Chapman chose this life for most of his seventy-one years. He learned the language of the birds, and he befriended wild animals. For his dinner, he might collect nuts, cranberries, mushrooms, and cattail roots. Sometimes John would come upon a pioneer family and have a meal with them. But if meat were served, he would excuse himself politely—a meat stew meant killing an animal.

3 What picture do you form of John Chapman based on these details?

4 John Chapman was born in 1774 in the village of Leominster, Massachusetts, just before the Revolutionary War for Independence from Britain began. It was autumn, the time of year when apples are harvested and cider is made.

4 What facts do you learn about Chapman in this paragraph?

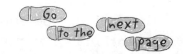

GUIDE TO READING THE SELECTIONS AND THE QUESTIONS

● **POINTS TO NOTICE**

When he was about six, John's family moved southwest to Longmeadow, Massachusetts. The young boy probably learned his letters in a one-room schoolhouse and spent Sundays in worship.

❺ In the 1790s, the United States included the eastern states and land south of the Great Lakes and west to the Mississippi. The Northwest Territory—the land west of Pennsylvania between the Ohio and Mississippi rivers—was just opening up for settlement. Men who had fought in the Revolutionary War were seeking new opportunities and heading west. John Chapman, now a young man, decided to join them.

John took with him little more than his knowledge of planting apple orchards and his faith. His religion was new to America, and was based on the teachings of Emanuel Swedenborg. Swedenborg was a scientist, philosopher,[1] and theologian.[2] He believed that God was in every living thing and that good deeds should be done because this was the way of God. John lived his life **❻** according to these principles. He would not intentionally[3] hurt any living thing, and he gave freely to those less fortunate than himself.

❼ John dedicated his life to helping people. He planted apple orchards so families who followed him out west would have food. He read to families he visited from a book about religion, or left religious passages or books with them. He loved children and would talk to them and listen to their stories. He gained the respect of the Indians **❽** he met as he traveled the woods and rivers of the new territories.

❾ John gathered apple seeds whenever he could. Sometimes he collected them from cider mills. He would separate the seeds from the apple pulp, then wash and dry them. He walked the land that pioneers would eventually come to and planted orchards for their benefit.

❺ Why did John Chapman decide to travel west?

❻ Put these two principles in your own words.

❼ Summarize the information in this paragraph.

❽ Why do you think the Native Americans Chapman met would have respected him?

❾ How would Chapman's planting orchards help the settlers?

---

[1] **philosopher:** a person who studies truth and wisdom

[2] **theologian:** a person who studies religion

[3] **intentionally:** on purpose

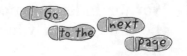
Go to the next page

| GUIDE TO READING THE SELECTIONS AND THE QUESTIONS | ● POINTS TO NOTICE |

If John came upon a pioneer family at a time that was not right for planting, he might leave a bag of seeds with them. The children would always want to know how long it would be until the seeds turned into apples.

John planted trees wherever he went, usually in clearings near rivers or streams. He surrounded his plantings with natural fences to keep animals away.

Sometimes he let the trees grow right where he had planted them. But usually he'd return after two years and take the saplings, pack them carefully, and leave them at a way station, with a family, or at an inn, in exchange for clothing, food, or money. Sometimes he gave the trees away.

⑩ John Chapman planted thousands of apple trees as far west as Indiana. His unusual ways, kindness, and giving heart made him known to pioneers he had never met. You might know him by his other, more popular name: Johnny Appleseed.

⑩ Why did people Chapman had never met come to know about him?

Go to the next page

GUIDE TO READING THE SELECTIONS AND THE QUESTIONS

● **POINTS TO NOTICE**

❶ 33. The chart below shows two principles John Chapman lived by. Complete the chart, giving examples of how he put each principle into action.

Principle

Principle	
People should not intentionally hurt any living things.	
People should give freely to others less fortunate than themselves.	

❷ Before you start to answer this question, think about what these principles mean. Then look back at the article to find examples.

❷ Make sure you answer both parts of this chart. Be as complete as you can. Make sure you use specific examples from the selection in your answer.

❸ 34. John Chapman became known as Johnny Appleseed—a true folk hero. Why did Chapman become a hero to people?

_____

_____

_____

_____

❸ Before you start to answer this question, think about what makes a folk hero. Then think about the things Chapman did. Remember to use specific examples in your answer.

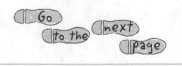
Go to the next page

Arbor[1] Day Celebrates Our Love of Trees

America's love of trees is still strong and growing. Every year the United States celebrates Arbor Day, a national holiday that had its beginnings in Nebraska.

According to the holiday's founder, Julius Sterling Morton: "Other holidays repose[2] upon the past; Arbor Day
(14) proposes[3] for the future."

(15) (16) Like John Chapman, Morton came west to grow trees. The trees he planted on the Nebraska plains would help block mighty winds, keep moisture in the soil, and provide shade, lumber, fuel, and food. Morton urged others to grow trees. But it wasn't until he proposed that one day each year be set aside to honor tree planting that his idea caught on.

On the first celebration of Arbor Day, in 1872, more than a million trees were planted in Nebraska. Arbor Day became a legal holiday in Nebraska on April 22, 1885, the anniversary of Morton's birth. In other states and throughout the world, Arbor Day is observed on different dates,
(17) depending on the best times to plant trees.

Children planting trees for Arbor Day

---

[1] **arbor:** tree; a place surrounded by trees

[2] **repose:** rest; look toward; put trust in

[3] **proposes:** builds a plan for

(14) **Look at the footnotes. They will help you understand the meaning of his words.**

(15) **What is the connection between John Chapman and Morton?**

(16) **This paragraph gives you some important information. Why did he plant trees?**

(17) **Make sure you understand this last sentence. Why is the best time to plant trees different in different parts of the country?**

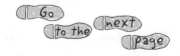

GUIDE TO READING THE SELECTIONS AND THE QUESTIONS

● POINTS TO NOTICE

National Arbor Day is the last Friday in April. The chart below shows the month when each state celebrates Arbor Day.

⓲ November	Hawaii	
December	South Carolina	
January	Florida	Louisiana
February	Alabama Mississippi	Georgia
March	Arkansas Kansas North Carolina Tennessee	California New Mexico Oklahoma
⓳ April	Arizona Connecticut Idaho Indiana Kentucky Michigan Missouri Nebraska New Hampshire New York Oregon Rhode Island Texas Virginia West Virginia Wyoming	Colorado Delaware Illinois Iowa Maryland Minnesota Montana Nevada New Jersey Ohio Pennsylvania South Dakota Utah Washington Wisconsin
May	Alaska North Dakota Vermont	Maine Massachusetts (April 28–May 5)

⓲ Why do you think people in Hawaii celebrate Arbor Day at a different time from the rest of the country?

⓳ When do people in New York celebrate Arbor Day?

Go to the next page

GUIDE TO READING THE SELECTIONS AND THE QUESTIONS

POINTS TO NOTICE

20 35. Explain Julius Sterling Morton's words, "Other holidays repose in the past; Arbor Day proposes for the future."

_____

_____

_____

_____

_____

_____

_____

20 To answer this question, put Morton's words in your own words. Think about holidays you know that look toward the past. Use these as examples in your answer. Tell how Arbor Day looks toward the future.

ACTIVITY

Directions Practice for the test by answering Questions 33, 34, and 35. Go back to the articles as often as you need to. Make sure you include specific details and examples in your answers.

Self Evaluation

Ask yourself

✸ Did I answer the question?

✸ Did I say what I think clearly?

✸ Did I organize my ideas well?

✸ Did I use specific details and examples?

✸ Is my writing interesting?

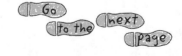

LESSON 3   How Your Answer Will Be Marked

What makes a good answer? Think about what you have been learning in Unit 2. Teachers will use the same rubrics to mark your answers as they did in Chapter 4. Take another look at what these rubrics look like. The rubrics on pages 190-191 are similar to the ones teachers will use. Then look at the sample responses on pages 192-193.

Rubric
The Graphic Organizer

4	3	2	1	0
✱ is complete	✱ is brief	✱ may be incomplete	✱ is incomplete	✱ does not answer the question
✱ contains correct information and shows understanding	✱ shows some understanding	✱ may show that the story is not really understood	✱ is inaccurate	✱ is wrong
				✱ does not make sense

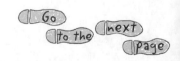
Go to the next page

The Short Answer

4	3	2	1	0
✿ answers all parts of the question	✿ answers most of the question	✿ answers some of the question	✿ answers only a small part of the question	✿ does not answer the question
✿ shows an understanding of the theme or key elements	✿ addresses some of the key parts of the story	✿ shows understanding of only part of the theme or key elements	✿ misses important parts of the story	✿ is wrong
✿ shows insight	✿ shows a mostly literal understanding	✿ shows some misunderstanding of the story	✿ shows only a little understanding	✿ does not make sense
✿ makes many connections to life and experiences	✿ makes some connections	✿ makes few connections to life and experiences	✿ makes no connections	
✿ uses examples from the story to provide good support for the main idea	✿ provides less support	✿ does not contain enough support	✿ may contain details that do not support the main idea	
✿ has no mistakes in grammar, spelling, punctuation, and capitalization	✿ has no mistakes that interfere with meaning in grammar, spelling, capitalization, and punctuation	✿ has some mistakes in grammar, spelling, punctuation, and capitalization	✿ has several mistakes in grammar, spelling, punctuation, and capitalization	

Sample Answers

Question

33. The chart below shows two principles John Chapman lived by. Complete the chart, giving examples of how he put each principle into action.

Answer

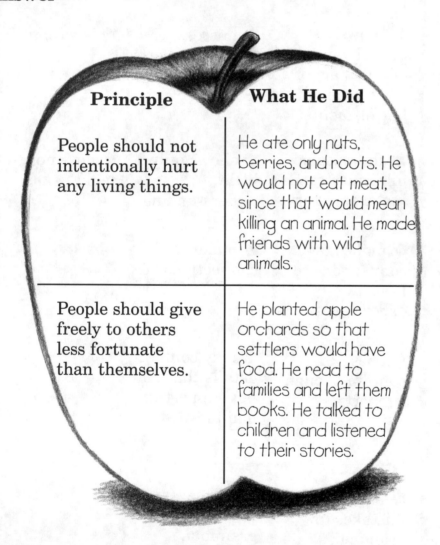

Principle	What He Did
People should not intentionally hurt any living things.	He ate only nuts, berries, and roots. He would not eat meat, since that would mean killing an animal. He made friends with wild animals.
People should give freely to others less fortunate than themselves.	He planted apple orchards so that settlers would have food. He read to families and left them books. He talked to children and listened to their stories.

Comments

This shows what a 4 response looks like. Both parts of the assignment are filled in. There are many examples from the story, and all of these examples show how John Chapman turned his principles into actions.

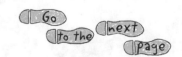

Question

34. John Chapman became known as Johnny Appleseed—a true folk hero. Why did Chapman become a hero to people?

Answer

Usually, a folk hero is someone who does extraordinary things. John Chapman was extraordinary in two ways. First, his behavior was very unusual. He had wild animals as friends, ate only nuts and berries, and lived in the woods. The kindness he showed to people was remarkable. He planted apple trees so people would have food to eat. He planted trees wherever he went and he left seeds behind with children. Stories about him traveled around because of the way he acted and because of all the trees he planted. These stories turned him into an American folk hero.

Comments

This answer also shows what a 4 response looks like. It answers the question fully. First it explains what a folk hero is. Then it tells the two ways that Chapman acted like a folk hero. It uses examples from the story to support the main idea. The ideas are organized well and the response is well written.

Question

35. Explain Julius Sterling Morton's words, "Other holidays repose in the past; Arbor Day proposes for the future."

Answer

Holidays such as Thanksgiving and Memorial Day honor events from the past. They give us time to think about these events and understand why they were important. Arbor Day does not honor an event from the past. Instead, it makes us think about the future. The trees we plant will benefit people and the land for a long time.

Comments

This is a very nice answer and it receives a 4. It discusses both parts of the quotation. It uses specific examples—Thanksgiving and Memorial Day—to support the writer's main idea.

LESSON 4 How to Write a Long Answer

You have read two articles and answered questions about each one. Now you are going to show that you know how to connect information and ideas from both articles. You are also going to show that you know not only how to read for facts, but also how to read with understanding.

Keys to Success

These strategies will help you be successful when you write your answer. On page 196, you will put these strategies to work.

When you write,

Plan

Use the planning page. Brainstorm and organize your ideas before you write. Ask yourself: Have I come up with some good ideas? Have I organized my ideas?

Make Connections

Remember that your task was to read two selections, not just one. In your answer, make sure you talk about both stories. Use details and examples from both. Ask yourself: Have I made connections between the articles? Have I shown that I understood both of them?

Stay Focused

Make sure that every sentence in your answer supports the main idea. Cut out any details that do not. Ask yourself: Have I stayed focused on my main idea?

Show Style

Revise and edit your answer. Pay attention to your style. See if you could have said something better. See if your answer flows smoothly. Ask yourself: Have I varied my sentences and my vocabulary? Is my answer clear? Is it easy to read?

Be Correct

Leave time to proofread your answer. Make sure you correct any errors in grammar, spelling, capitalization, and punctuation. Ask yourself: Have I corrected all mistakes?

Go to the next page

GUIDE TO READING THE QUESTION

1 36. You have learned a lot about two special people—John
2 Chapman and Julius Sterling Morton. Use examples
and details from both articles to tell

3 ✱ how they are similar

✱ how they are different

4 ✱ what makes them both special

5 Proofread your writing to correct any errors in
spelling, punctuation, capitalization, and grammar.

_____

_____

_____

_____

_____

_____

_____

_____

_____

_____

_____

_____

_____

_____

_____

🔴 POINTS TO NOTICE

1 You are going to write about two people.

2 Make sure you use examples and details about both people.

3 This prompt is asking you to compare and contrast. Decide how you will organize your answer. You might have one paragraph show how they are similar and one show how they are different.

4 Conclude your response by showing what makes them special.

5 Remember this important step: Proofread.

Go to the next page

_____

_____

_____

_____

_____

_____

_____

_____

_____

_____

ACTIVITY

Directions **Write an answer to the question. Plan your writing on a separate piece of paper.**

Self Evaluation

Ask yourself

Did I stick to the topic?

Is my answer well organized?

Did I connect my ideas?

Did I use vivid language?

Did I vary my sentences and vocabulary?

Is my writing interesting?

Did I proofread my writing?

Teachers will look for the same qualities in your long answer that they looked for in your short answer. They will also look for several other factors. Take a minute to review the rubric for judging your long response. Then look at the sample answer showing you what a 4 looks like. This is what you should reach for—a top answer!

Rubric
The Long Answer

4	3	2	1	0
✱ keeps to the topic	✱ may contain a few details that do not fit the topic	✱ tries to stay focused on the topic but contains details that do not connect	✱ may contain many details that do not connect to the topic	✱ does not fit the topic
✱ is well organized	✱ is somewhat organized	✱ shows some attempt at organization	✱ shows little or no organization	✱ is not correct
✱ is well written, using vivid language and interesting sentences	✱ is somewhat easy-to-read, using mainly short sentences and basic vocabulary	✱ is not very interesting, using only simple sentences and basic vocabulary	✱ uses only simple words and sentences and contains sentence fragments	

Go to the next page

Sample Long Answer

Question

36. You have learned a lot about two special people—John Chapman and Julius Sterling Morton. Use examples and details from both articles to tell

   ✽ how they are similar

   ✽ how they are different

   ✽ what makes them both special

   Proofread your writing to correct any errors in spelling, punctuation, capitalization, and grammar.

Answer

What makes a person special? Is it that the person has done something remarkable? Is it that the person has changed the world? Or is it simply that the person has left the world a somewhat better place to live in? In the case of John Chapman and Julius Sterling Morton, we can say: "The world is a better place because of what they did!"

Both men felt it was important to plant trees. John Chapman is better known by the name Johnny Appleseed. He traveled around the country planting apple trees. He traveled as far west as Indiana and wherever he went he planted apple trees. He also gave seeds to others

Go to the next page

so that they could plant apple trees, too. Julius Sterling Morton was responsible for planting many trees, too. Like Johnny Appleseed, he encouraged others to plant trees. He even created a national holiday for trees.

   The reasons these men planted trees were different. Johnny Appleseed wanted to help people, while Morton wanted to help the environment. Johnny Appleseed wanted to make sure that settlers who came to the new frontier would find food to eat. He gave them seeds so that they could plant their own apple trees. Morton knew that trees would help the land. He planted them to block the winds. He planted them to help keep the soil moist so it wouldn't blow away. Also he planted them so that they would provide fuel and timber and food.

   Both men achieved their dreams and live on in our imagination. John Chapman lives on through tales of that American folk hero, Johnny Appleseed. Morton lives on whenever we celebrate Arbor Day—a holiday he began. Most importantly, they live on when we look at the beautiful trees that cover this country.

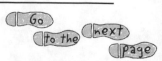
Go to the next page

ACTIVITY

Directions Try to judge this sample answer yourself. Work with a partner. Discuss each of these questions.

1. Does the response have a strong beginning, middle, and end?

_____

_____

2. Does this response answer all parts of the question?

_____

_____

3. Does this response keep focused on the topic?

_____

_____

4. Is this response well organized?

_____

_____

5. Does this response include specific details and examples from both articles?

_____

_____

6. Is this response well written and easy to read?

_____

_____

7. Does this response contain errors in grammar?

_____

_____

8. Does this response contain errors in spelling, capitalization, or punctuation?

_____

_____

Remember This!

• • • • • • • • • • • • •

When you proofread, check your grammar. Correct any errors before you turn in your writing.

Proofreading Marks

Add a word or words	∧
Take out a word or words	℘
Change a word	two ~~one~~
Start a new paragraph	¶
Add a period	⊙
Add a comma	∧
Change the spelling	believe ~~beleve~~
Capitalize a letter	=
Lowercase a letter	⫽

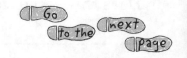

ACTIVITY

Directions **Proofread the passage below. It contains ten errors in grammar. The first one is corrected for you.**

My aunt May lives in Texas. Whenever she comes to visit us, She tells my brother Bob and I stories about Pecos Bill. Pecos Bill was the biggest, stronger, and meanest cowboy you can imagine he had wild bears and wildcats as friends when he was growing up. Bill is raised by coyotes. Hunting with them and speaking their language. When he was a fully grown man. He had a fight with a rattlesnake. He fought so hard, the rattler begs for mercy. From then on, Bill used the rattler as a rope to catch cows and Gila monsters. He also fought a mountain lion after he beat the mountain lion, the giant cat agreed to wear a saddle. And let Bill ride him. Bill rode the mountain lion until he found his horse Widow Maker.

LESSON 7 Proofread for Mechanics

Remember This!

● ● ● ● ● ● ● ● ● ● ●

Before you turn in your writing, check that you have spelled every word correctly. Check that you have used the correct punctuation marks. Check that you have capitalized correctly. Fix any mistakes so that they don't take away from your score.

Proofreading Marks

Add a word or words	$\wedge$
Take out a word or words	ℐ
Change a word	two ~~one~~
Start a new paragraph	¶
Add a period	⊙
Add a comma	∧
Change the spelling	believe ~~beleve~~
Capitalize a letter	≡
Lowercase a letter	ⱷ

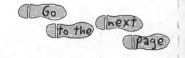

   Measuring Up™ to the New York State Learning Standards

TIME
OUT
FOR
SKILLS

ACTIVITY

Directions **Proofread the passage below. It contains ten errors in spelling, punctuation, and capitalization. The first one is done for you.**

Pecos bill once tried to ride a cyclone up in kansas. The cyclone reared and bucked as though it were a hoarse. It tried to throw Bill from it's back. What a fight Bill put up? Finally, the cyclone just rained out under Bill. The reign pounded down so hard that it formed the grand canyon. Bill landed in california in the spot we now call Death valley. This was the only battle Bill ever lost!

LESSON 8   Apply to the Test

You've been practicing your proofreading skills. Now apply them to the test. Read the prompt below. Then proofread the sample response.

Question

36. In "Apple-Seed Man," you learned that John Chapman planted apple trees to benefit, or aid, the pioneers who would come to the new territory. Explain how the trees would aid the pioneers.

Proofread your writing to correct any errors in spelling, grammar, punctuation, and capitalization.

Answer

The trees aded the pioneers in severel ways. The fruit from the

trees gave them somethings to eat. The pioneers plants the seeds

from the fruit. And grew more trees. Also the trees provided shade

from the sun. And fuel for there fires the trees also looked

beautiful. Johnny Appleseed traveled from massachussets to

indiana. And planted apple trees all along the way.

$\mathcal{D}$*irections*
Read the article, "How Wildflowers Get Their Names," and an entry from the National Audubon Society's *First Field Guide: Wildflowers*. Then answer the questions.

How Wild Flowers Get Their Names

by Jennifer Ewing

Have you ever seen a lady's slipper or a shooting star? These are not your mother's shoe or a bright light in the dark sky. These are names of wild flowers. The petals of the shooting star blast out in every direction from the center of the flower, and a lady's slipper looks as though it could fit on a very small foot. There's a lot of imagination used in naming wild flowers.

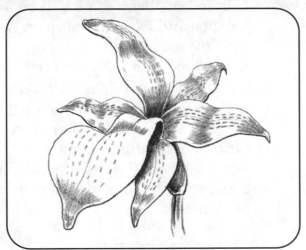

Lady Slipper

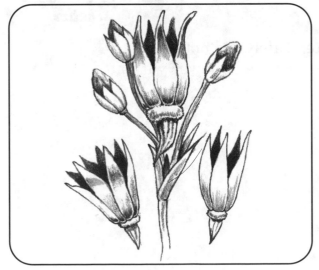

Only in a field of wild flowers might you find a cluster[1] of blue witches next to a row of Chinese houses. What do you think baby blue eyes or pussy paws look like? Little elephant-heads have flowers that look like two big ears and the trunk of an elephant. If you use your imagination, you can see the eyes and beak of an owl in the flower of the owl's clover. If

---

[1] **cluster:** group

Go On

you pinch the toadflax flower, the frog mouth opens. These wild flowers are all names for the way they look.

Some wildflowers got their names because of the way they were used. Coyote tobacco was smoked and chewed (but not by coyotes). You can eat some wild flowers.[2] Miners lettuce was eaten by miners (and American Indians). Wild strawberries might taste good on shortcake. Cow parsnip is a tasty herb for cattle.

The story of how the forget-me-not got its name is a sad story about love. Two lovers were walking along the Danube, a river in Germany. The girl saw some beautiful blue flowers growing along the bank. She asked her sweetheart to pick them for her. They were growing on a very steep bank, which was dangerous to climb. He didn't want to disappoint her and climbed the bank to pick them for her. He lost his balance and fell into the river. As he fell, he threw the flowers up onto the bank. As he was sinking under the water, he called out, "Forget me not."

These kinds of names make it easier to identify and remember some of the many types of wild flowers. Wild flowers often have different nicknames in different parts of the United States. If you have wild flowers around your house, try to come up with your own names for them. Use your imagination.

Pussy Toes

Toadflax

_____

[2] Not all wild flowers can be eaten safely. Do not eat wildflowers on your own. Never eat a wildflower without getting an expert's advice.

Go On

33. Use examples from the article to complete this chart.

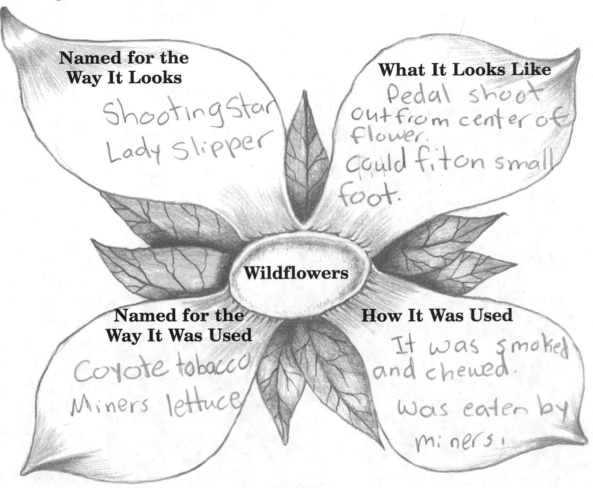

Named for the Way It Looks

Shooting Star
Lady Slipper

What It Looks Like

Pedal shoot out from center of flower.
Could fit on small foot.

Wildflowers

Named for the Way It Was Used

Coyote tobacco
Miners lettuce

How It Was Used

It was smoked and chewed.
Was eaten by miners.

34. Read this sentence from the article.

There's a lot of imagination used in naming wildflowers.

How does this article about wild flowers show that this statement is true?

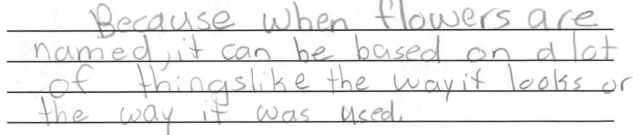

Because when flowers are named, it can be based on a lot of things like the way it looks or the way it was used.

Go On

From *National Audubon Society First Field Guide: Wildflowers*

TRUE FORGET-ME-NOT
Myosotis scorpioides

Legend has it that a suitor was tragically[1] lost in a raging current as he tried to pick this flower for his love. His last words to her were "Forget me not!" Forget him, she never did.

LOOK FOR: Small sky-blue flowers with yellow center. Hairy stem divides into 2 branches near the top, separating as the flowers bloom.

LEAVES: 1-2 inches long; oblong, hairy

HEIGHT: 6-24 inches

BLOOMS: May-October

HABITAT[2]: Wet places

RANGE: Widespread

[1] **tragically:** very sad; unfortunate
[2] **habitat:** place and natural conditions where

Go On

36. What can you tell about the habitat of forget-me-nots
    based on the information in this article?

It blooms from May-October
in wet places. Some grow by the
banks near water

Go On

Planning Page

Use this page to plan your writing for Number 36. Do not write your answer here.

By what they look like
By what it is used for.
I agree with the author
because lots of flowers dont
look alike
Shooting star-by look
Lady slipper-by look
Coyote tobacco - by what does
miners lettuce-by what does

Go On

212 English Language Arts • Level D   Copying is illegal.   Measuring Up™ to the New York State Learning Standards

36. In "How Wild Flowers Get Their Names," the author says, "these kinds of names make it easier to identify and remember some of the many types of wild flowers." Tell whether you agree or disagree with this statement. Include

    how wild flowers get their names

    whether or not you agree with the author's statement

    specific details and examples from both articles.

Proofread your writing to correct grammar, spelling, punctuation, and capitalization.

Wild flowers got their names in 2 ways, the way the look and what it does. The Shooting Star and the Lady Slipper flower both are based on the way The petals of the shooting star blast out from every direction from the center of the flower. The lady slipper looks as though it could fit on a very small foot. The Coyote Tobacco and the Miners lettuce are named on the was it was used. The Coyote Tobacco was smoked and chewed. The Miners Lettuce was eaten by miners.

I agree with the authors statement because if you know what the flower looks like or how it is used, then you will identify it quicker.

Go On

English Language Arts • Level D   Copying is illegal.   Measuring Up™ to the New York State Learning Standards

ACTIVITIES

 Reading

Like Johnny Appleseed, Paul Bunyan and John Henry are legendary folk heroes who many believe were based on real-life people. Find out more about one of these two heroes or choose another folk hero. Make notes as you read on the lines below. Then share your findings with your classmates.

_____

_____

_____

_____

_____

_____

 Listening

Imagine you are taking a younger brother or sister or cousin to a folktelling contest. What tips would you give this youngster for listening to the folk tales. Write your tips on the lines below.

_____

_____

_____

_____

_____

_____

ACTIVITIES

 ## Writing

You can find out more about Arbor Day by writing for information to The National Arbor Day Foundation. Their address is 100 Arbor Avenue, Nebraska City, NE 68410. Write questions you would like answered by this foundation on the lines below.

_____

_____

_____

_____

_____

_____

Speaking

The state tree of New York is the sugar maple. Do some research to find out why this tree was chosen as the state tree. Write your findings on the lines below. Prepare a presentation to share your findings with your classmates. Also tell them if you agree or disagree with the choice.

_____

_____

_____

_____

_____

_____

_____

Measuring Up™ to the New York State Learning Standards

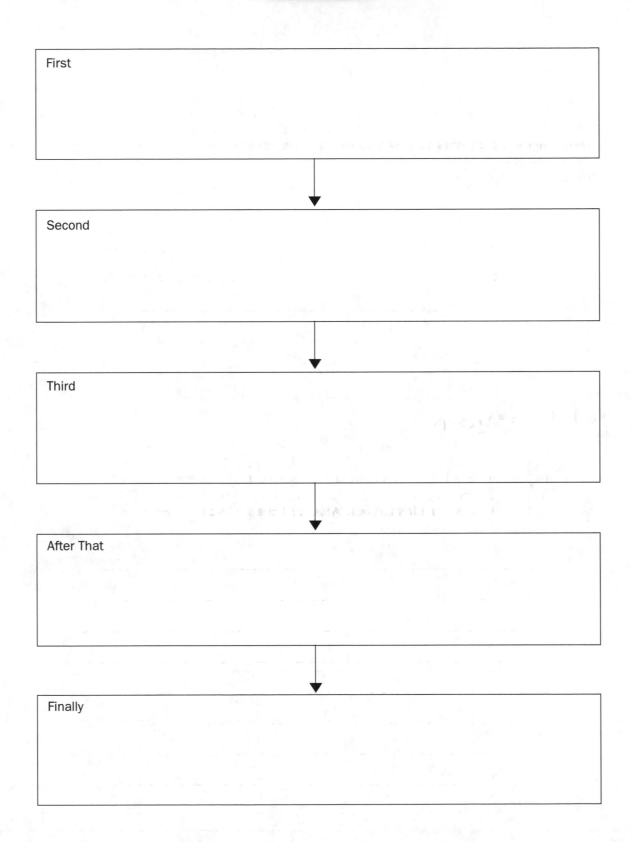

First

Second

Third

After That

Finally

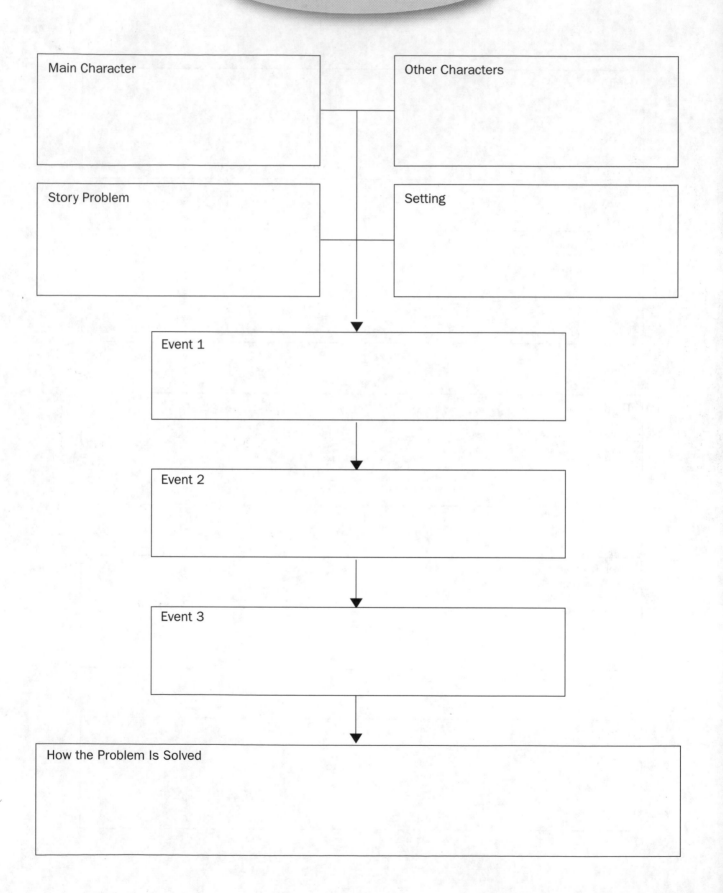

Main Character

Other Characters

Story Problem

Setting

Event 1

Event 2

Event 3

How the Problem Is Solved